KV-397-095

Paul was one of those people I'd vaguely known for years before anything actually happened between us. When we were younger, we used to hang out in a huge group together. I'd really liked Paul then but nothing had come of it. Gradually, we'd all drifted into other friendships. Then two Christmases ago, my close friend Josie decided to throw a party and, out of the blue, Paul and his mates arrived. I was immediately informed of how great he was looking and, with extra courage provided by the weird and wonderful punch Josie was serving, went over to chat to him. We spent the rest of the evening talking to one another. A friend told me later that you could literally see the sparks crackling between us...

from The Women's Press

Jane Waghorn has taught English and drama at a number of London secondary schools over the last seventeen years, and at the Sixth Form Centre, which is part of The Community College Hackney, since 1989. She lives in Stoke Newington, North London, with her husband and two daughters.

Through Thick and Thin

Young Women Talk Relationships
Jane Waghorn, editor

To Cleo and Abigail

First published by Livewire Books, The Women's Press Ltd, 1996
A member of the Namara Group
34 Great Sutton Street, London EC1V 0DX

Collection copyright © Jane Waghorn 1996

The copyright in each of the pieces in this collection remains with the original copyright holder.

The right of Jane Waghorn and the contributors to be identified as the authors of this work has been asserted by them in accordance with the Copyright, Designs and Patents Act 1988.

British Library Cataloguing-in-Publication Data
A catalogue record for this book is available from the British Library

This book is sold subject to the condition that it shall not, by way of trade or otherwise, be lent, re-sold, hired out, or otherwise circulated without the Publisher's prior consent in any form of binding or cover other than that in which it is published and without a similar condition including this condition being imposed on the subsequent purchaser.

ISBN 0 7043 4940 X

Typeset in Bembo 11pt/13pt by Intype Ltd
Printed and bound in Great Britain by BPC Paperbacks Ltd

Contents

Acknowledgements

I would like to thank all the contributors to this book. Laurie Critchley, at The Women's Press, was a constant source of inspiration, and my editing partner for this project. Henrietta Davies, and Di Middleton helped me enormously with their practical and emotional support. Ian Williamson sustained me by recognising the value of this book from the outset. My parents' encouragement over the telephone made me think about my own times as a younger woman, and how much I cherish my relationship with them.

Introduction

Like a great many women, I am inquisitive and fascinated by other people's relationships. In part, this is because I want to feel that my own experiences are not too different from others'; it is comforting to hear some of my thoughts and feelings echoed in the words of others. It is also because I want to know as much about other people as possible.

So I was keen to compile a collection of writing about relationships; it seemed like a great opportunity to feed my interest and to hear about what I think is really important. Young women, in particular, enjoy and are good at writing about themselves – their writing often reflects the richness of their experiences and they are very worldly wise – and so I was particularly delighted to be asked to edit an anthology of young women writing on this subject.

Even though I knew how powerful and intense

1

young women's writing is, when I started to receive submissions for this book, I was struck by the sheer strength and quality of the writing. The willingness of the contributors to share their private worlds and to candidly discuss their personal relationships was remarkable. Some of the contributions were difficult to read because they were so full of hate or sadness or fear. Some pieces were started but not finished because the writer found it too painful to continue. The pieces in this book have been chosen because they show a tremendous range of emotions and experiences, and because, as well as exploring the complexities and difficulties of relationships, they share a quality of connectedness and warmth. Despite problems and painful times, the writers here care a great deal about their families and friends and lovers. They display a depth of feeling and understanding rarely noted or respected by older adults.

For me, my conversations and interaction with all the young women who submitted pieces have been the highlight of this project. It has been a privilege to move into their worlds for a little while; to listen to what is really going on — and to learn from it.

Jane Waghorn

Sisters

Big Sis

My big sister Sarah is my only sister (thank God). She is twenty-five years old, seven years older than me. It's taken us many years to really get on as when we were younger, we didn't have much time for each other because of the big age gap between us. Well, to be honest, she never had much time for me.

Sarah and I never went to school together. This meant I was never seen as her 'little sister' but was always treated as an individual by the outside world, which was good. Despite this, Sarah had a huge influence on my ideas, my style and my tastes. This was probably because when I was young we moved to the other side of town. I was too far away to play with my school friends, so the only people I saw were my parents and Sarah. I always wanted to hang out with Sarah and her friends. But we never spent much time together out of school either: Sarah would always be out or, if her friends were over, she'd shut them in her room. When I tried to join them, she'd shout at me and jam the door closed. I was always treated as the pesky 'baby sister' and never just as 'Laura'.

This meant that I never really knew what she was up to. It would drive me crazy. I was always dying to find out what Sarah did and who she was doing it with. In the end, I started to sneak into her bedroom when she wasn't there to read her diary. Sarah never realised I knew where it was (in the left-hand drawer of her desk) and when she reads this she'll probably want to kill me. Sarah's diary taught me a lot: about boyfriends, drinking and partying. I also discovered that she smoked. After that, I'd try and find her cigarettes as well. Seeing as she wouldn't tell me anything, I guess I felt that the only way of ever finding things out was to go through her room.

When Sarah turned eighteen, she left home for a job in London as she didn't want to go to university. Being the younger sister I think I was supposed to say 'hooray' at finally having the house to myself. But in reality I was gutted. It was a nightmare. Even though we weren't the best of friends – as you can see – I really missed her. It was weird not having her around. It was growing-up time but my big sister wasn't there when I needed to talk about boyfriends, periods, etc.

I became very bitter, especially when Sarah came home to Cornwall for holidays. I hated the way she would look down on everyone and boast about where she'd been and what new clothes she had. I was always having a go at her about treating our home like a hotel (which she did). She still never spent any time with me, even though we often didn't see each other for six months or more. She still wouldn't take me anywhere, with her friends or going shopping, or even to the cinema. In some ways I was jealous and this was probably the worst stage in our relationship.

I did get some good things out of Sarah living in London, I suppose. I think it made me more open-minded and gave me a wider perspective on things. I also became more cultural, and would know about new bands and new fashions before anyone else at school did. I always knew what was 'in' at the time because Sarah would tell me.

A couple of years later, Sarah fell on hard times and moved back home. I was really looking forward to having the family back together again. What a mistake. Sarah hadn't changed a bit and I felt like I was seven years old again and lumbered with Mother Number Two. She thought she knew it all and patronised me in everything I did, what I wore, what I said, even what clubs I went to. I'd grown used to getting all the attention from Mum and Dad, and that was difficult too. To make it worse, Sarah was really good at making me look like the 'baddie'. Luckily after eight months of near hell, she moved back to London again.

Our relationship grew stronger when Sarah moved to London. I'm not sure why. Perhaps I just grew up and appreciated what she wanted to do more. I suppose I was old enough now to understand her better. Anyway, I would write and phone her regularly, and we talked more, which was brilliant. When she came back to Cornwall to visit, we began to go out to the pub or out clubbing together. For the first time, we started getting on like two friends.

We've had this kind of relationship now for a couple

of years, and recently it's got even better. Last August, I found out I'd be going to Bristol University. I was really excited: I'd be living on my own and meeting loads of new people. I couldn't wait. After I moved, I realised that Sarah had been through what I was going through: new house, new friends, new life. I understood now why she hardly ever came back home after she first moved to London. Too much to do in your own place.

Now that I'm in Bristol, London's only two hours away by train so Sarah and I see each other more often. The last time I visited her in London, we went shopping together. Sarah paid for lunch and we went out for drinks in the evening. It was lush. Sarah made me feel very welcome and the whole visit was really relaxed.

Last month, we passed an even more important stage in our relationship – for me, at least. After thousands of phonecalls and naggings on paper, Sarah made the effort to come and see me in Bristol. Even though I'd been hassling her to visit, when she finally agreed to come, I was nervous. I didn't know what to do with her – especially as she's always moaning that she has no money. Finally, I decided to take her windowshopping on Saturday. I treated her to lunch and got tickets to see an up-and-coming band that evening. (I also ended up lending her sixty pounds to buy two new tops, which she still owes me the money for.)

For me, the weekend was important because I needed to prove to Sarah that I could do it too: that I was able to live on my own and lead my own life. But more than that, it was a great weekend and I think

Sarah really enjoyed herself. These days I feel closer to Sarah every time I see her, and I think she feels the same way too.

Laura Wasley

Seven Sisters

Being eighteen in the 90s is tough enough, but dealing with seven demanding sisters on a daily basis adds to the challenge. My position as the eldest daughter has meant that I've learnt the hard way that I can't get everything I want – especially where my parents are concerned. It has also meant that I have a thorough understanding of the words 'responsibility' and 'patience'.

By some miracle, the relationship I have with my sisters is on the whole very good. But to get even one of them to admit they like me would be virtually impossible. (There seems to be some unspoken rule out there that confessing to liking an older brother or sister is guaranteed to cause abject humiliation.) This ungrateful attitude that my sisters have towards me can be frustrating considering how demanding my job as the eldest can be.

Let me tell you, for example, how my seven-year-old sister Nasrena behaves when she comes home from school every day. As soon as I open the door, she grabs me round the waist, starts swinging, and repeats three times, 'I hate you, I really, really hate you.' Her twin, Rushena, also treats me like a human roundabout. I'd like to think this is just the twins' way of saying they appreciate me. But this interpretation of their behaviour is wearing thin as I get a very hard time from them *and* from my parents if I don't carry out their every whim.

My parents expect me to play games with my younger sisters whenever they want me to, believing that this is the only way to keep them calm and that I can always do my homework later. It's no big surprise then that I have considerable problems trying to keep them all happy, quiet and entertained. They, on the other hand, find it impossible *not* to annoy me.

The sister who made my job the most difficult when she was younger was my third sister, Rehana. From the age of five months she has been what I consider a problem child. She has always refused to partake in the process of peaceful negotiation, preferring confron- tation or out-and-out war. When she was seven she got angry with me for changing the TV channel without consulting her and decided to empty all the household rubbish on to the living room floor.

At the time, logic told me that since Rehana was the one who emptied the bin, she should be the one to clear it up. As a thirteen-year-old, I did not realise that my parents didn't think logically when allocating blame. According to them, I was the one picking on – and I quote – 'your innocent helpless seven-year-old sister'. Innocent was the last thing Rehana was. Luckily her temper has diminished slightly now that she's reached the grand old age of twelve, but through all those other ages, I was the one who suffered.

(The irony of all this is that it's now Rehana who can't stand any untidiness in the house and she is the first one to get the house clean. She is also the one who gets on my nerves the least – for now, that is.)

One particular thing that I like about my relationship with my sisters is that they feel comfortable talking to me. So I hear fascinating revelations about everything that occurred that day at school, from the latest about the so-called teacher who eats cat food to who's going out with who. Other riveting news includes what new swear words now exist in the English language and who the school bully is. All these titbits of information, as you can imagine, are mesmerising.

The real problem with all this communication is that my sisters just won't stop telling me things. I sit there for hours trying to look interested, when what I'd really like to do is scream into a pillow. I *am* interested in what they do at school, it's just there's only so much one can take. I'd much prefer them to talk about school with my parents, which would mean I'd stop having to repeat all their conversations, but this rarely happens.

The other difficulty with encouraging my sisters to talk is that they all feel they are bound by some law to point out every mistake I have ever made as well as all my flaws. I am told by my five-year-old sister, Rumana, who I otherwise get along well with, that I shout too much. I would love to inform her that I am on the verge of finishing my A Levels and need a little peace and quiet to avoid killing myself. But I can't. If I even mentioned the words, she would instantly tell my parents I was about to commit suicide. Sometimes this does seem an easy escape, but my priority would be to kill Rumana first.

Although I'm only kidding, any teenager with a sibling under the age of seven knows there's a fine line between joking and actually committing murder for a little peace and quiet. I hate having to constantly explain to my sisters that 'No, I can't help you with this project and no, I can't play that game, because I also have school work to finish'. They forget all the times I *do* play with them and badger me constantly, saying 'You're never around . . .' and 'You don't ever play with us . . .' In the end, I inevitably have the words, 'You think you're so big now' thrown in my face.

Rubena (my eleven-year-old sister) and Regena (who's nine) are, out of all my sisters, my worst nightmare. They have at this young age perfected the art of playing havoc with my emotions. At home, they are also the two who have been in trouble so many times it's not worth mentioning. There are two reasons for this: they are both highly opinionated and neither knows when to keep her mouth shut. While Rubena continues to criticise my dress sense – her favourite phrase with a look of disgust is 'you're not wearing *that* are you?' – Regena manages to go one better and oversee the destruction of all my personal belongings. When the twins decided they were going to scribble all over my school text book, Regena decided to watch them do it. Only after the book was totally destroyed did she come and tell me that 'the twins did it'.

Rubena and Regena have, as a team, managed to get me to promise them *anything*, just so they will stay away from me. They can have exclusive use of the video, read my books and help themselves to my belongings, for this small, but essential, concession. Of course what really annoys me about these two is that they are perfect angels at school as well as being good students. It's just when they get home that they undergo this negative transformation. I don't mind if they misbehave, but they do it *all* the time and all their efforts are focused on *me*.

It's mainly because of Rubena and Regena that – contrary to what my parents believe – I feel like I have no control over my sisters. Whenever I try to assert any authority, their usual response is not to take me seriously. 'We don't have to listen to you!' they laugh. The only times they both pay attention to me is when I start shouting and ordering them about, as they know perfectly well that when I'm in this mood, I will involve my parents. I *hate* shouting and getting angry, but I'm stuck in a no-win situation.

My parents expect me to act like an adult and to magically discipline all my sisters when they misbehave. My sisters, on the other hand, hate me when I turn into a 'parent' and refuse to even acknowledge me. I remember when I told on Nasrena for destroying my schoolwork and she got into trouble with my parents. In revenge, she got all her comrades together and the little monsters sent me to Coventry for over an hour until they needed something from me. Basically, if I act like my parents, I upset my sisters, but if I don't, I upset my parents. In the end, no matter how much

I try to balance these two roles, I'm never very successful.

I do have an ally of sorts in Hena, my fifteen-year-old sister. I can't stand some of her mannerisms and her tone sometimes and she can't stand mine. But she is the one person out of all my sisters who I can talk to and the one person who really listens and takes me seriously. Hena and I have been through a lot together and are very close.

When my mother came over here from Bangladesh, she was only seventeen and spoke no English. It was hard for me as the only child but then, when Hena came along, we took turns comforting and looking after each other. We both like reading and we have talked about books together from a very early age. Hena knows me better than even my parents. This has nothing to do with her age but a lot to do with her personality.

Unlike my other sisters, Hena is quiet at school *and* quiet at home, as well as being extremely intelligent and trustworthy. Yet this doesn't stop her from having a temper that has to be seen to be believed. Even though I get on with her, I hate having to calm her down when she gets into a rage. Unfortunately, I have to – and take her physical abuse if necessary – as everyone else is afraid to go near her.

I admire the way Hena is taken seriously by everyone in my family. At the same time, I envy the fact that everyone takes a softly-softly approach with her. I think the tension in our relationship arises when I realise that she gets a lot less trouble from my younger sisters than I do. This has nothing to do with them appreciating her more, and everything to do with how much they fear her.

You would have to be superhuman to keep the peace in our house, but I often resent Hena's quick temper. This is because Hena doesn't realise how tough my job is. She refuses to take any responsibility for my younger sisters and I get really annoyed with her for not taking some of the pressure off me. The worst thing is I don't think she ever will. Some of this has to do with the fact that she isn't able to get through to my younger sisters unless she's in one of her more violent rages. I, on the other hand, can't afford to get as angry with my sisters as Hena does.

Instead, I'm probably the main reason why there haven't been many problems between my seven sisters. They all find it easier to take their anger out on me. Getting mad at me means they don't take it out on each other, which would mean a lot of punching and crying. (Luckily with me it's all verbal.) I, in turn, have learnt to take on the chaos they cause and deal with it so that it doesn't become a huge problem.

Somehow, through this, I've also become the official family negotiator between my parents and my sisters. Recently, Hena was invited to join a 'Choice Club' in Clapton. A 'Choice Club' is somewhere you learn everything you need to know about going to university. Dad wasn't keen on Hena going so I had to negotiate on her behalf. I explained what a good idea it was and how all her teachers wanted her to attend. Eventually, my parents agreed, but sadly it was too late for Hena to get a place by then.

What upsets me most about this is having to act like a third parent and attend numerous parent–teacher evenings that go on for ever. Just the other week, I went to a parents' night for Rumana. At the moment, she's having problems speaking at school. She won't talk to people or mix with her friends. It's up to me to explain this to my parents and try to sort it out. Sometimes the responsibility feels too much.

What's worse of course is that I end up feeling guilty for getting annoyed about these things. It doesn't matter how upset I get or how many times I use the phrase, 'it's not fair', it all boils down to one thing: my parents speak English less fluently than me, therefore I have to take on a lot more responsibility than would otherwise be expected.

My parents have made it quite clear to me that I am responsible for all of my sisters now, and I will continue to be so after they have gone. This of course comes as no surprise as I am from an Asian background in which the eldest daughter or son is usually responsible for the family. For me to say to my parents 'I'm tired of looking after them when I can barely look after myself' is unthinkable. It's not a situation that I can personally opt out of. I do get tired sometimes but everyone has bad days.

One thing I have lost out on by having so many sisters is privacy. Unless I am out of the house, I am surrounded by sisters, day and night. I don't consider myself an especially fascinating or interesting person, yet my sisters are convinced that they must follow me wherever I go, or else they will miss out on some riveting conversation or, even worse, some fun. It drives me crazy at times, but as I've grown older, I've got more used to this and see being surrounded by sisters as part of normal life.

It does get difficult though when my friends come round. It doesn't matter how many times I say 'GO AWAY', my sisters never listen. They know my friends almost as well as I do and consider them to be their friends too. This means they think they have as much right to be around my friends as I do. I know it sounds absurd to get so wound up about sharing my friends (and I *am* glad my friends get on with my sisters). But I have to share almost every other aspect of my life with them, and sometimes it feels as though not even my friends are my own.

I have also lost out on a social life because of my sisters. My parents are strict about me going out anyway, but I rarely get the chance to leave the house as there is always some crisis or other that needs sorting out. I used to get angry about this, but now like everything else, it has become a normal part of my life.

I know it may seem that I should be tougher with my sisters and a bit more demanding where my parents are concerned. But issues like having a social life aren't taken very seriously in my family. I doubt I could get my point across to my parents anyway as I don't speak Bengali very well. I have told them, as well as my sisters (now that they're older) that I need some space to myself once in a while and, more recently, I've been given it. But I feel that to continue with the 'it's not fair' routine would be immature and so I've moved away from that and tried to make the best of what I've got. I do find my role as the 'eldest child' daunting at times. It's as if my future's been planned out for me. But I wouldn't trade my situation for anything. For a start, even though my sisters give me trouble, they are also unusually loyal.

Once, when I was picking Regena up from school, one of her friends asked if I was married. Regena said no and her friend went on to say that I looked like I was married. Regena was furious. How dare the girl say this, she exclaimed, and then she told her that I was going to be a lawyer and be rich. She acted as if the girl had insulted me. I was very surprised to discover that Regena believed I was destined to be more than someone's wife as, until then, I thought she had no opinion about my future other than to take care of her.

The person I am today is due to my family. I have become very resilient, determined and patient, and I'm not scared of responsibility. It is also because of them that I can cope with almost anything thrown at me. I am also lucky to have a close group of friends who, like my family, stand by me. They are prepared to listen to me complaining when things get bad, so I don't explode.

Because I *am* the eldest girl I know my responsibilities and accept them. I feel too strongly about 'family' to ever consider not fulfilling them, and I love my parents and sisters too much. What I love most about having sisters is knowing that I'm needed and important to my family.

Nina Miah

Sister

I hate my sister. I absolutely hate her. Give me a gun and I'll probably shoot her. Actually, I don't hate her *that* much. But if you had a sister like mine, you'd know what I am talking about. Any ordinary sister–sister relationship has its advantages and disadvantages I admit, but this relationship is an all-round disadvantage. Every day and night, we're at each other's throats.

One major reason why my sister and I fight all the time is that we both have to sleep in the same room. This is a living hell because I am an asthmatic and my sister is a light sleeper. Even if I make the slightest sniffle, or just breathe a little heavily, she'll be straight out of her bed to hurl abuse at me.

I can understand how she feels because I can't stand it either when people breathe heavily in their sleep. But I have to put up with her talking in her sleep, and sometimes she really scares me. Once she started talking in a Scottish accent – that really freaked me out.

The arguments my sister and I have at night are definitely the most aggressive and violent ones we have. We almost always end up waking up the rest of the house. Sometimes when I get up in the morning and remember what I said to my sister the night before, I can hardly believe it. Sometimes, it really makes me want to laugh. Sometimes though we can both say things that make each other cry, even though what we're fighting about is really silly.

I suppose my sister and I *are* very close in a way – and sometimes it seems as though we both *do* really want to get along. But for some reason or another, we'll probably start arguing again. For example, my sister will often try to be nice to me when I happen to be in a bad mood. Then I'll end up becoming even *more* irritated because she's being nice. Sometimes it's the other way round. I might be nice to her, but she ends up jumping down my throat for no reason at all. Often it seems that the only way for my sister and I *not* to fight is for us to avoid each other completely and only speak to each other if we really have to.

Sometimes, however, and this is on very rare occasions, we'll both get on with each other. When this happens, we almost end up treating each other in an extra nice way. This usually takes too much energy out of me though, so it only lasts for about an hour or so. Then we start getting on each other's nerves again. But it's nice while it lasts.

When my sister and I do get on with each other, we normally talk about clothes or make-up or hairstyles – very girly-type things – like most sisters probably do.

21

I suppose one of the reasons why these conversations don't last long is because we have very different tastes. I'm a person who loves to go shopping, spending money, and trying on different outfits and styles, whereas my sister is more conservative. We'll start arguing about how much money I spend on clothes or about me buying clothes that my parents won't approve of. She's just such a sensible person.

Because I enjoy fashion, I often make up different hairstyles for different occasions. I'm very good at it and I do it for other people too if they're going out somewhere special. But for some reason – I don't know why – I can never bring myself to help my sister with her hair, or suggest styles she could use, even though she asks me to. I guess I just enjoy annoying her by doing things like that. It makes me feel better.

In a way, *all* the arguments I have with my sister make me feel better. It's a way of letting my anger out on someone. Fortunately, I have my sister around to be that someone. Most of the time I find it really easy to provoke her into losing her temper. I really know how to wind her up, even if it's just for a laugh.

The result is that my sister and I can never go anywhere alone – we'd probably end up killing each other. I'm sure this is what my mother believes because she always tries to ensure that we are never left at home on our own together. Even when our eldest sister got married, we ended up arguing over something really silly. (That time, though, it definitely wasn't my fault.) My cousin wanted a camera to use for the wedding so I gave him mine. When my sister found out that I'd given my camera away and wasn't taking pictures myself, she shouted at me in front of everyone and then slapped me. Maybe I made a mistake but my sister embarrassed me in front of everyone by over-reacting, and the hurt I felt then is still there.

If I was ever going to try and stop arguing with my sister it would be for my parents' sake. My mother is always asking me not to be provoked by my sister, or if I provoke her, not to carry on the argument. A few months back, before my parents went on holiday, the *only* thing they asked us before leaving the house was not to argue. That's when I realised that our arguing was affecting them a great deal. Now both my sister and I try not to argue in front of them any more.

If we do argue in front of my mum and dad, they almost always take my side – probably because I'm the youngest. (It doesn't seem to matter whether I'm in the right or wrong.) At times I feel quite bad for my sister because she's the only one who gets into trouble when we fight. My parents feel that because she is older she should be able to control her temper better than me.

The problem is that my sister's really impulsive. She doesn't have much self-control, and will sometimes end up blurting things out she doesn't mean. But she can also keep secrets and is a person you can confide in. Although I don't do this very often. I know, though, that I can rely on her not to tell my parents about certain things I've done.

Underneath, my sister is probably a really nice person. She is good to my parents and I know there is still room for us both to mature. I have a feeling that eventually we will stop arguing, perhaps when we get married or start to lead separate lives.

Sara Khan

Brothers

Living with the Fiend

When he was born, I liked him. But tastes change. At first, he was 'our' baby. He smelled sweet, and like a bee hypnotised by a flower I was enchanted by his tiny fingers, tiny toes, tiny nose. The tiny ears just like mine and those tiny eyes which seemed to shine. He was real, not like the plastic baby dolls I used to play with.

I was five years old when he was born. I don't really remember Mum being pregnant, just being different: fat. One moment it was the three of us and then from out of nowhere came a little bundle of joy . . . or not as the case may be. An extra body needs extra space, so naturally we moved, leaving Sam – my dog and best friend – at a nearby farm. Obviously I was a little distressed at losing Sam, but still being excited about a baby brother, I thought it was a fair deal. However, I was wrong.

As he grew so did the mess and chaos which was permanently around him. In the summer a dozen or so flies could be seen hovering around his head like a halo. These were his friends along with the worms, spiders and ants which he spoke to in the usual, cute babble that babies use. Mum was endlessly trying to keep him clean – and our bath times together became a daily ritual. Anything that moved went into the bath, my Sindy doll, his cars, tanks and soldiers, as well as a bottle or two of bubble bath. We were always swamped in bubbles which we used to make beards and funny hairdos with. It was fun. Then when it was time to jump out we'd protest in unison. I guess we were what mum calls 'Water babies'.

Yet he still proved to be a thorn in my side and a continuous source of embarrassment. Take for instance my ninth birthday party when he decided to put a strawberry gâteau – my birthday cake – on his head. To others this may seem funny and thinking about it now it was, but at the time I was mortified and wanted the earth to swallow me up. He sat there with his face covered in almonds and some red sticky stuff trickling down his head. I just couldn't believe he'd shown me up by behaving like such a baby! What would my friends in their spotless party dresses think? By Monday I was sure to be the class reject, the loner with no pals and it was all because of him. All I wanted to do was stab him, shoot him, send him to Timbuktu, *anything*, just so that I never had to see him again.

These sorts of feelings never disappeared completely but subsided every now and then. It's strange that although I sometimes wanted him punished, I couldn't bear to see him smacked. I even took some of the whacks for him – Mum would chase us around the sofa armed with a slipper and before she could hit him I'd jump in between acting as a shield. Maybe it was because he was so small and looked like an angel (when he was asleep) that I took on the role of protector. He needed someone he could depend on, someone who'd fight all the baddies in the world. Perhaps I'd watched Wonderwoman too much but I wanted to take care of him. This was especially true when our parents argued, and I'd crawl into his bed, taking him in my arms. I'd try and protect him from the screaming and smashing of plates. He was fragile and needed care which I assumed responsibility for. This wasn't completely welcomed by him; he didn't need two mothers telling him off and smacking him for eating bogies, a delicacy he relished.

Now he often complains in a bitter voice, 'Shut up, you're not my mother.' Defensive, I respond with some witty comment that hides my hurt. Maybe it's just hard to let go. He doesn't need me, perhaps he never did. But I no longer recognise him as the cute and innocent child he once was. Over the last two years he has become a fiend, an awful monster who lurks in your worst nightmare.

A teenager oozing with testosterone he needs someone to focus his anger on I suppose, and that's me. Of course his argument is with the rest of the world, I'm just a good substitute for the boy who kicked him on the bus or his English teacher or even my mother.

If I disagree about what to watch on tv, he'll hurl

the controls at me. If I lose my temper and shout at him, he'll retaliate by breaking my things. I'd eaten his yoghurt so naturally I deserved to be punched. I'm only a head taller than him now and he's still growing and getting stronger.

I do retaliate and sometimes I think I could kill him, but I'm no murderer, so I retreat into my room. To him this is a victory. But why does he feel the need to act like this?

Perhaps I created this fiend by bossing him about when he was a child. But I don't think this is true. I don't think I was ever that bad to him. I may have told him off and been too protective but I thought I was just being a good big sister.

The real problem is his attitude. He treats my mum and me with no respect, and he's even beginning to treat my dad this way too. What if he grows up to treat other people like this?

My mum is really worried about him, but she always gives into him and that makes him worse. If he hits me or is rude to her or Dad, she'll ground him but then let him off. In the end he always gets what he wants.

I wish Mum and Dad knew what to do, but I guess like most children I'm expecting too much from them. After all we didn't come with a users' manual. Seeing them not being able to control him, though, makes me feel powerless and frightened.

According to a friend who was once in a similar position, the fiend is part of a 'natural' process of boys growing up. Believe me, this does *not* feel natural. However I'm willing to hang on to the hope that perhaps when he reaches twenty, we'll be able to have a civil conversation. Him though – my little brother – I will always miss.

Kelly Indaco

Robbie

My parents are Mark and Mary Austin. I don't call them my 'foster parents' or my 'other parents' because I was adopted when I was three days old and to me, they're the one and only set of parents I've got.

The same goes for my brother, Robbie. Or Robert McKay Austin in full. Robbie came to live with us when he was five years old and I was seven. I remember that we'd been looking for a younger brother for me for some time. One day I came home and my mum told me they'd met a boy called Robbie and that we were all going to meet him. At the time, the thought of sharing my parents with someone new didn't really bother me because all previous attempts at finding a brother had fallen through. Besides, I was quite young then and nothing ever *really* bothered me.

We arrived at the house where Robbie was living on a school day, Friday actually. As I said, I wasn't bothered about meeting Robbie, just pleased to be having a day off school. I remember walking into the house and seeing him for the first time. I've never been to see a newborn baby brother or sister in hospital, so I don't know whether it would be similar to the way I felt then. It was like, 'here's my brother-to-be.' But I imagine it wouldn't be quite the same as if your brother or sister's just been born because you aren't starting from scratch — foster children are already people, who have been through a lot before you have met them. When I first saw Robbie, though, I didn't really have time to think about all that. I just thought, 'My God!'

I don't know what I was expecting of Robbie, but I remember thinking, 'this is no ordinary five-year-old'. I remember watching him play with all the toys on the floor and saying to myself, 'I don't want this boy, I don't like this boy'. To be honest I hated the whole place. Looking back now, I feel disgusted with myself because a lot of the children there had learning difficulties like Robbie. Many of them had also had difficulties with their families, and here I was, coming from a good home and going to a great school, turning my nose up at this foster home. I have always tried to justify myself by saying that I was only young and that anyone would have reacted the same way I did, but I still feel guilty.

We all came out of the foster home — Mark, Mary, Robbie and me — and stood on the pavement. It was so strange and different — if things worked out as my parents hoped, everything we did now would be for a group of four not three. 'Table for four please!' I can't really describe the feeling I had, but you'll know what

I mean if someone new has ever been added to your family. It's like your whole life is changing and you don't know whether you like it or not. It's weird.

Anyway, on that first day, we all went to Docklands Light Railway for the day. Robbie was so quiet and well behaved, you'd never have recognised him if you knew him now. It was like hanging out with the living dead at times. You'd ask him a question and he'd either ignore it or answer as simply as possible. When Robbie first came to live with us, his range of vocabulary was very small and it's nice to see how it's grown. Also he's become much more confident about speaking which is good. After our outing that day, we took Robbie back to his foster home where he lived with his foster parents and fifteen other children. I remember leaving in kind of a daze. I still couldn't believe Robbie was going to be my new brother.

The next day, Saturday 2nd December 1989, we went back to see Robbie. We were going to have a 'trial session' together. This meant Robbie would come to stay with us for a while just to see how we all got on. We'd already decorated his room – it was toy-town yellow with Thomas the Tank Engine curtains and bedspread. Robbie went straight to bed as soon as he was told. In fact, at the beginning, Robbie did anything we said immediately. He was always neat and tidy and he'd make his bed every day. (I still don't know what's involved in making a bed.)

Robbie hated getting his hands and clothes dirty, which is odd because your average five-year-old loves to get dirty. If any of his clothes got dirty, he'd cry and run upstairs to change; and if his hands got sticky, he'd hold them away from him or curled them into fists.

We had a special dinner when Robbie first came to us because he was picky about what food he liked. I think it was sausages and ice-cream.

After Robbie had gone to bed that night, we three stayed up and spent the whole evening talking about him. I complained about everything possible – from the way he spoke to the clothes he wore. I'd never say those things now, but I suppose I still hadn't got used to 'the four of us'. Not surprising really as I'd only met him the day before.

Mum and Dad were always optimistic and kind about Robbie. 'The poor lad can't help his jacket, Julia!' they told me. But I also didn't quite understand about Robbie's learning difficulties. For a while, I remember thinking that he was faking everything. I couldn't believe that anyone could do things so slowly. Every night I'd creep outside his bedroom door and try to see if he was doing something that would give him away. I don't know what I was listening for – maybe a report to Orson like in *Mork and Mindy*. But I truly thought Robbie was pretending and that he could really speak exactly like I did. It sounds dumb, but that's what I thought.

Fifteen days after Robbie came to us, he celebrated his sixth birthday. All our family came to tea and they brought toys and presents. I remember feeling really jealous. I felt angry every time someone gave him a present. I kept on thinking, 'those presents should be mine!' and I was glad when my aunt brought a special present just for me.

My mum took six months off work to look after Robbie because although he'd gone to school at his foster home, he'd missed out a great deal. Every day

35

when I came home from school, Mum and Robbie would tell me where they had been that day and what they'd done. I felt so jealous and angry. I never cried, but I'd look at Robbie and think, 'Why does he deserve all the attention? It's not fair. I'm still here, everybody, don't ignore me!'

It was a really hard time for everyone. It was frustrating for Mum because she was used to working, and I was upset because while I went to school, Robbie went to the zoo. Of course, it wasn't all outings and laughter, but I still resented him.

Now, things are totally different between Robbie and me. I no longer feel the resentment I did, and we're much more of an ordinary brother and sister team. Of course no brother and sister get along one hundred per cent of the time, but I feel we're more average siblings now. There are, however, differences between us and a 'normal' brother and sister, mainly because of our mental differences. Although he's only two years younger than me, I can't enjoy a film with Robbie or have an in-depth discussion with him in the same way that most siblings can.

At times Robbie can be really kind and caring. Sometimes if a day has gone badly for me, I'll go to Robbie and he'll care and offer me chocolate and hugs. Don't get the idea that he's a saint though. Robbie can be one of the most painful people I've *ever* known. Like when he refuses to wear his sandals outside. Every school day in summer we have huge arguments about this, which include a great deal of kicking and screaming. Eventually, he puts the sandals on. Once, though, he tried the same thing on at my Auntie's. Everyone babied him and called me a 'meanie'. Robbie sat there pouting and said, 'she always bosses me about and kicks me'. Of course everyone looked at me and tutted. I could have stabbed him then.

On the whole I think Robbie is a great brother. I think it's awful what he's been through – but I won't go into his background because it's personal. I also think, in the long run, that siblings are good for you. They teach you how to share and relate to people. All in all, I'm very happy with Robbie and me and the way things have worked out, even though we inevitably have our occasional hiccups.

Julia Austin

Mothers

Mum, Darran and Me

I want to tell you about my mum because for the last fifteen years, she has brought me and Darran, my brother, up by herself.

My mum was born in Hackney and lived here until she got married in 1972, when both she and my dad moved to Chatham in Kent. My brother was born in 1977 and I was born a year later. Things didn't work out between my mum and dad, so when I was two years old, Mum told my dad to leave. She was worried that if they tried to stay together, Darran and I would suffer because of the bad arguments.

I think Mum was brave to get a divorce from my dad and carry on with life, bringing me and Darran up alone (without my dad visiting or paying maintenance). She sold the house we had in Kent, and we moved back to Hackney. We lived with my nan and grandad for about a year, and then moved into a three-bedroom flat about five minutes' walk from them.

Darran and I went to primary school whilst Mum did a part-time job to help with food and clothes. Then, when I was about eight, she started college to train to be a Nursery Nurse. She got her NNEB and now works in an infant school. She's been working full-time for seven or eight years. Looking back, I think that my mum had great determination – that is one thing I admire. She was able to go to college full-time and work at home in the evening while still bringing up two children almost single-handedly.

People seem to think that if you are in a single-parent family, you must have a bad relationship with that parent. I've told people that I don't see my dad, and they say, 'Oh . . . I'm sorry' as if there's been a death in the family or something. You see children who get into trouble on the television or in the newspaper, and they always seem to mention that they are living with a single mother. Maybe I'm just paranoid and, because I'm in a single-parent family, I notice it more. I can understand people moaning when women get themselves pregnant just to get a flat. I think that's wrong. But when I hear something against *all* single mothers, it really annoys me.

My relationship with my mum is very good. If I have any problems or worries, I can go and tell her about them. Mum is very open-minded, and she talks to Darran and me openly about issues like sex and drugs and things like that. She makes us feel it is all right to talk to her about anything.

My mum isn't strict, but you always know where the line is that you do not cross. I can't remember her smacking me. I know she has a couple of times, but she never did it unless it was really necessary. I hate it when I see people – it is usually mothers – smacking their children along the street. I've even heard parents say that they will smack their child with a slipper when they get home. I really don't like that, and I'm glad my mum would never do anything like that because it would be *very* embarrassing!

Another thing about my mum is the fact that even now she still buys food or clothes for me and Darran before she even thinks about buying something for herself. For example, she still wears clothes that she's had for the whole of my life, even though it's only around the house. I might need an extra pair of jeans, while she needs a coat, a pair of shoes and a skirt, but she will still go out and buy jeans for me and not even think about the fact that she's only got one pair of shoes. I suppose you could say that the way she acts is good because I get more clothes. I don't mind that, but I hate seeing Mum go out and buy something for me or Darran when she needs far more stuff herself. I especially hate it now that Darran and I probably have more spending money than she does.

All this probably makes my mum sound like 'the perfect mum' but as with all parents, there are some problems. What really does annoy me about her is the fact that she can be so over-protective of both Darran and me. When I first started wanting to go out with my friends, Mum wouldn't want me to go. I must have been about twelve years old before I first went out with my mates from school. We went ice-skating and Mum took a lot of persuading to let me go. Only a couple of months ago, I wasn't allowed to go into the West End at night to go to the cinema. I have managed to persuade Mum to let me go to the cinema at night, but only to the one in Holloway which is nearer.

Mum and I usually argue over silly things like going out with friends. Other things we argue about are stupid things like drying the dishes or going to bed when it's late. Mum worries about me riding my bike on the road, and when I first got my bike we had lots of arguments over whether I should wear a helmet. I wear one now because I ride on the road, but Mum made me wear one just so I could go out with my cousins on their bikes. This year I was allowed to go to France for a week, but I was with three adults as well as three people the same age as me, including my brother Darran.

Darran and I are only thirteen months apart in age, so we have grown up together really. I don't think Darran can remember life without me. We are very close. Mum laughs at us because one minute we are having a huge argument, shouting at each other, and the next minute, we will be sitting somewhere and laughing about nothing in particular. I suppose it's good really that we can't stay angry at each other for more than two hours.

I hear so much about people who don't get on with their brother or sister. They either have lots of arguments or they never talk. I usually just sit and listen to what they have to say about it, unable to say too much about Darran, just the fact that he doesn't listen to me when he gets something wrong – he just says, 'Shut up!'

I wouldn't say that we had a perfect brother–sister

44

relationship, nobody does. It's just that the disagreements we have are usually so small that we forget about them in five minutes. It is just the little things that Darran does that annoy me – are you reading this, Darran? Like when he says something under his breath, because he wants you to hear him but not what he is saying. Sometimes he talks to me and I have to ask him to repeat himself because he speaks so softly, but that is Darran, he is very quiet . . . most of the time!

It is difficult for Darran in some ways because our dad is not around. I remember when he first started to shave. It was quite difficult because Mum wasn't sure what to get him to shave with. My mum's two brothers were good because they both spoke to him and gave him ideas about what to use. Darran also looks a lot like my dad. It's funny though because if he does something, like moan a lot, my mum will say, 'You remind me of your father' and he absolutely *hates* it! I usually remind him of the fact myself, just to wind him up.

People think that because my dad isn't around, Darran might try to 'Dad me around'. I don't think he could be bothered doing that. He is quite protective of me, but he doesn't try to tell me what is right or wrong. I think it's because we are only thirteen months apart and he doesn't notice the difference in age that he doesn't feel he needs to treat me like a dad would. (I'm not sure if he thinks he has to try to be the 'man of the house' or not.)

I think my mum sometimes finds it difficult being both Mum and Dad though, because there are times when she wants to talk to someone else besides Darran and me. I think she would like another 'adult' around at times. But it is better now because she can have a reasonable conversation with us, which she couldn't do when we were only five and six years old.

Darran remembers when our dad left, I think that is his only real memory of him. I don't remember him at all. I think this makes a very slight difference to the way we both are now. When we were younger though, my mum says that Darran used to be *very* quiet, which she puts down to the arguments she and my dad used to have. Also after my dad left until I was about two-and-a-half to three years old, Mum says that I was very nervous (which I don't remember). But once I started nursery school, I was fine. I think that even though our dad is not around, Darran and I are well adjusted to life in 'the big wide world'.

In general, my relationship with both Mum and Darran is very good. I think I am one of the lucky ones, because I've had quite a happy childhood and have never had any real reason to say otherwise.

Stacey Faulkner

A Day in My Life
with My Mother

Monday, 10 July
11.20pm

I am in my room writing this. My sister Luthfa is in
her first stages of sleep from the looks of it. Uncle
Masroor is in our house, visiting from Belgium with
two other male relatives. When they arrived this evening, Dad as usual asked me to go and help Mum out
in the kitchen. I was annoyed by this, though I know
I shouldn't have been. It's just that I *always* get asked
because I'm a girl – or maybe it's because I'm the
eldest child and there is no one else to ask. As it is,
I'm not even that much help to Mum as I don't know
how to cook curries or deserts or prepare anything
special for guests. I just end up washing dirty dishes,
cleaning the meat or vegetables, keeping an eye on
what she's cooking, giving it a stir, and setting the

table. Secretly, I resent the pressure that as a young woman, I should know how to cook; the expectation that I should be able to pick the skills up 'naturally' and enjoy cooking without a problem.

Mum really appreciates my help, though, and even if I wish it wasn't expected of me, I also wish I could do more. I have promised myself that I will learn how to make everything she cooks over the summer holiday. It's a promise I've been making myself for the last two years.

I had woken up this morning around nine o'clock and found that everyone else was already awake except for my mother and baby sister. Mum had been up at dawn for early morning prayers as usual, but recently my sister has been keeping her up late into the nights because she is teething. They're both always catching up on sleep these days.

My dad made breakfast for us. I washed my youngest brother, and then my younger sisters, brothers and I all had breakfast together and tidied up as Dad set off for work.

'Have you had your breakfast?' Mum asked the minute she woke up. It was good to be able to answer yes.

Mum didn't smile, but her eyes softened and she wanted to know what my brothers and sisters had eaten. I told her what they'd had. She was pleased I could tell. This was our longest conversation of the morning.

I cannot recall a time in my life when my mother and I have talked heartily with each other. Our conversations are always brief and superficial because my mother is always busy with work around the house and with looking after my younger brothers and sisters. Even when I was a small child, the few moments I would spend with her would be during prayer time at dusk. Mum would sit me by her prayer mat while she quietly recited verses from the Qur'ān. After finishing her prayers, she would sit near the open door and look out into the yard which you could barely see in the darkness, quietly murmuring more verses. Her voice was so low that it sounded as if she was humming a song.

(These days I'm not even sure how accurate this memory is because I was only three years old at the time. But it is so vivid and fresh in my memory that I think it must be true. I also remember Mum doing this with my sister Farhana who was born a year later and with my brother, Rezaal, who was born after Farhana's fourth birthday.)

Even when we do have some time together, I usually feel very uneasy talking openly with Mum. I have trouble expressing my true feelings and emotions – and I think Mum feels the same way. Even as a child I always kept my distance. I remember when my maternal grandmother died. I was seven years old back then and fully understood the meaning of death. I watched my mother cry with my baby brother in her arms. I had been deeply hurt by the news of grandmother's death, but what hurt me most was seeing my mother cry. She was devastated. I wanted to comfort her, as I had seen my adult relatives do. I wanted to let her know that I was suffering too and that she was not alone. But I couldn't. I held back because I didn't know whether that was what she expected from me and I was afraid of her reaction. I now wish I had comforted her and told her about my loss, because for the next two weeks I cried on my own, away from Mum and everyone else.

At around midday today, after I'd finished tidying and vacuuming the house, my mother called me to help her in the kitchen. I immediately felt annoyed. The whole issue about food, my mother and me prays on my mind constantly because although I think my mother does want me to be independent in a way, she still believes that preparing and presenting food are a crucial part of being a woman. I get angry with her for this and I get angry with myself because I know that the situation would be very different if I was a son.

As with most Bengali families, my parents wanted a firstborn son. Because I am a girl, they sometimes feel cheated. This is not because they don't love me dearly, but because they feel the pressure of ensuring that I am able to learn and enjoy the traditional women's jobs, so that I can be successfully married and not become a financial burden to them.

Helping Mum prepare lunch meant that I was almost late for work. I didn't even have time to eat any of the food I'd helped her with, just grab a sandwich. I felt really cross. I have only been working for four weeks now, and this is my first job. For two years, I had been arguing with my parents to let me have a part-time job just for the holidays so it wouldn't interfere with my school work, but they wouldn't let me. The reason given was that our family had no need for money and that girls my age didn't need to go out to work. They felt it would be degrading to see their daughter working. Mum and Dad did eventually change their minds, but if I'd been a boy, I would have been *encouraged* to go to work, so that I could contribute financially to the family.

I finished work at five thirty. When I got home, Mum was taking a nap with my youngest sister. I was starving. In the kitchen, the table had been left set out for me. Everything was cold except for a pot of lamb curry with potato which was steaming hot. When I lifted the lid, I discovered that it was full which meant Mum had just finished cooking it for supper. I hated myself for being angry with her earlier.

After dinner, my younger sister and I helped Mum tidy up the kitchen. I had been wanting to speak to my mother about my cousin Hazera's marriage for some time. But marriage is a complicated subject so, since my sister was there and I wasn't feeling especially courageous, I didn't even attempt to bring it up. Instead I went to my room and rehearsed what I would say and how I would explain my concerns for my cousin.

It was not until nine thirty this evening that I found my mother in the kitchen on her own and could approach her about the subject of Hazera's marriage. Mum was heating a pot of vegetable curry for our guests. I looked around to see if there was anything I could do, but there wasn't. I decided to stand by the cooker and watch over the curry. After a minute's silence, I turned from the cooker and said, 'Will Hazera be studying in Bangladesh now that uncle and auntie have decided to settle down there?'

There was a warm smile on Mum's face but I couldn't read the meaning behind it. Did my mother understand the reasons for my concern? Or was her smile a sign of mockery? Was she laughing at me? Passing me a spoon, Mum replied, 'It's unlikely she'll study now that her parents have arranged her marriage.'

I began to stir the vegetables. 'You don't get an education only if you stay single,' I replied. 'They should at least consider letting Hazera finish her GCSEs in case at some point in her life she needs something to fall back on.'

'Why are you so worried about it?' Mum asked. 'If Hazera's parents don't know what is best for their own daughter, is there any point in you knowing?'

With this, Mum took the pot off the heat and set it on the table. I did not answer her even though I thought that yes, there *was* a point. Do she and Dad know what is best for me? Do they know how desperately I want to pass my A Levels and then get a degree in business or mathematics? That I intend to travel abroad to Far Eastern countries like Vietnam which is currently going through a major economic boom and has great potential for business investors?

It's at times like these that I really worry that my mother doesn't really know me or understand my needs and dreams. I want to do something meaningful and successful with my life and though I don't disagree with marriage, the thought of getting married before I've attained a stable career frightens me. My parents do want me to go to university, but deep inside I know they cannot guarantee my education because if a suitable marriage proposal comes along then they will be inclined to accept it.

I sometimes feel that my mother pities me. I'm not sure if this is because I am so ambitious or if she just pities me for being a woman. Probably both because it is very difficult for a woman to fulfill the ambitions I have and still stay within the framework of Bengali society. My mother probably feels that at the end of the day, my ambitions will add up to nothing and that the skill of cooking will be more useful to me than my GCSEs or A Levels.

But sometimes I feel that there is a part of my mother that admires me for being a Bengali woman and being so ambitious. This feeling of admiration is reflected when I'm staying up late revising for my maths test or trying to finish off an assignment. At around two or three o'clock in the morning, Mum will always look in on me and will ask me how much more work I have to do and when I plan to go to bed, if ever. Then she'll say that the teachers should take it easier on us. It is at times like this that I feel her love most.

Rubiya Begum

The Wasp and the Bee

The electronic organ accompanies the piano in uncertain harmony. There are maybe twenty or thirty members in the congregation today. I sit near the back, nodding and smiling at the faces I have always known. Standing by my side is a small woman: her eyes closed and her hands raised. Her joy in the presence of God transforms her and she appears ageless. It is not until I turn to look at her that I notice her face is weary.

My mother sees me watching her and smiles in return. Her smile is oddly shy – perhaps even a little apprehensive about her audience's response. I almost reach out for the hand which is now swaying by her side. But instead, I stand up too, smile, and join in hymn number 534.

Nothing much seems to have changed in this church in which I was brought up. Every Sunday for almost seventeen years I made the journey here with Mum.

So many Easters, Christmases and Junior Church weekends when I would be up the front reading, acting, even preaching while she looked on with pride. Now I return only as a visitor.

For Mum, the fact that I continued going to Church after my sixteenth birthday had been a cause for quiet rejoicing because both my brothers had fallen away from Christianity at this age. So my decision to leave just before I turned seventeen must have felt like even more of a betrayal. I tried to explain to Mum that I still believed in God, but that I needed to explore other ways of expressing my faith. But it wasn't difficult to see that my leaving the Church signified much, much more. For me, it was also a major step towards expressing my independence from her.

I don't want to give the impression that my mum interferes in my life, far from it. Still, for some time, I'd had a crazy feeling of claustrophobia which I just couldn't shake. It was mainly this that made me search for my own space away from Mum and the church. I just felt I couldn't tell Mum about how I was feeling without causing her further pain. But Mum's silent anxiety betrayed a sense of failure and loss more profound than I chose to acknowledge at the time. The church had been a strong bond between us, an umbilical cord. Now I desired to breathe alone.

My need for independence existed long before I turned seventeen. I remember making it quite clear to Mum, while I was still in primary school, that in future I'd be choosing my own clothes. I'd been teased that day about the dress I was wearing and with a child's brutal honesty, I explained to her that my black dress was only fit for a funeral while my blue frock made me look like a nun. I gave no thought to the fact that my words might hurt her. I just spoke the truth as I saw it.

Mum immediately granted me my freedom of choice. But she retained that most powerful of weapons, her opinion. Her advice, guided by practicality and expressed with maddening wisdom, always proved correct. More effective than a tribal dance, Mum's cautionary words 'it looks like it's going to rain' would inevitably guarantee that the heavens would open. I would always end up soaking wet after obstinately remaining umbrella–less and scantily dressed. (Mother Nature showing maternal solidarity I guess.)

Despite my refusal to take good advice, Mum has always said that 'an old head on young shoulders' is a fitting description for me. She says I never seemed newborn to her. She still recalls my birth with indulgent delight and holds firm in the conviction that I showed an uncommon sensitivity even then. Being her only daughter, I shared a special relationship with her and grew up to be her confidante, first in small ways then in large, perhaps before I was truly fit to be so. I remember the many occasions I watched as mouthfuls of bitterness rose like gall from deep inside her and she expressed a hurt with the world so profound that it resonated within my soul though I could hardly comprehend it.

It wasn't until just before I turned sixteen that I came to understand where these feelings came from. I finally convinced Mum to abandon the barricades of silence she'd erected so carefully to ensure her survival. I lay quietly in bed, my mum next to me in the position she customarily took for bedtime stories. But this time her tale did not caress me to sleep. It ignited a rage so strong that I burnt and choked till morning.

I won't tell her story here, but as her low voice calmly recited a catalogue of misuse and betrayed trust, I became completely numb. I could not conjure up a single soothing word and felt that by insisting that she tell me her history, I too was guilty of violation. Or maybe I was the one who felt violated by knowledge which I now wished vainly I had never acquired. Even as I attempted to come to terms with all I had heard, my subconscious worked selfishly to obliterate the details of her account from my memory. In the end, I was left only with a desire for revenge, made impotent not only by the passage of time but also by my pathetic inability to recall the very events which had provoked my fury.

That evening marked a turning point in our relationship. I've come to realise that though I'm aware of Mum's weaknesses, I hate to see them displayed. I lash out at each and every flaw which threatens my sense of her invincibility. A sore muscle or an aching back becomes a terrifying reminder of her advancing old age. Often I clog up with emotion which I can't put into words. Our mutual concern for each other's welfare is also sharpened by the fact that we share that uniquely cursed blessing: being born female and black. Sometimes our protective instincts lead to tensions in our relationship which can explode into fights.

I often feel now that I underestimated Mum's wisdom when I was growing up. I remember a cautionary tale which she used to tell me about the wasp and the bee. One day the wasp decided it wanted to learn how to make honey, so it went to the bee for help. The bee happily showed the wasp how to build a nest and make honeycomb. This proved a lengthy process and the wasp, irritated by his teacher's painstaking attention to detail, gave up on the lesson and resolved that he would go off and make honey alone. But try as he might, the wasp could not recreate the bee's magic. And to this day, whilst making very impressive honeycomb, the wasp has never been able to make honey.

For a long time, the moral of this fable was lost on me. Obviously, the wasp was stupid. Why didn't he just read a book about making honey? But now I realise that the story of the wasp and the bee was also the story of my mother and myself. I'd been brought up to value education as the key to future happiness, and I needed no encouragement to strive for good grades. I had no time, though, for the kind of learning which could not be judged at separate desks, under timed conditions, in the Great Hall at school. The sort of learning which I *could* gain from Mum. My 'good schooling' was a source of pride for her but it also created a rift between us.

Perhaps this feeling grew stronger as my seventeenth birthday approached. I'd become increasingly aware of Mum's dependence on me as the 'baby' of the family, and had been urging her, sometimes harshly, to stand on her own two feet. After all these years, my mum was suddenly faced with losing both her jobs at once. The factory where she'd been employed was relocating and now the last of her offspring wanted to relocate too.

The birth of my niece, Maxine, came just as I was

feeling really frustrated by the relationship between my mother and me. Maxine was a precious gift to me and even more so to my mother who became a grandmother for the first time. Suddenly, all our conversations revolved around babies: each gurgle, burp and tear a talking point. The whole family was enamoured with this peculiarly wilful and captivating child. Later when Mum began looking after Maxine while my brother and sister-in-law were at work, I breathed a huge sigh of relief.

The arrival of a new baby filled the gap which the old one – me – had left behind. Now Mum's beautiful voice sings lullabies and whispers words of wisdom once more, but to a new generation. It was strange though when my wish for more space became a reality and my return home from school was greeted with a nod rather than the grateful bear hug I'd come to expect. I even found myself occasionally resenting Maxine – the same niece who I had hoped for, prayed for and bored my friends rigid with stories about.

Struck by this paradox, I was forced to admit that the wealth of maturity which I so prided myself on was perhaps not so great after all. This knowledge and Maxine's arrival brought about a change in my relationship with my mother, opening up a new phase between us in which we can talk to one another woman to woman.

One evening this summer I especially remember. Mum and I sat on the iron mesh fire escape we used as a balcony, watching the sunset. I was fretting about my A-Level results and my future. Mum just assured me that everything would work out because God was with me. Although I've left the church, I envy Mum her certainty of faith while I am plagued by doubts. I keep trying to find a rational reason for everything, but turning faith into an intellectual exercise doesn't seem to work. Her real, loving and kind God seems so far removed from the impersonal theological concept I grapple with. I remember Mum laughed gently when I tried explaining this to her – comparing, I think, my minor worries with the troubles she's had. Like the evening sun, her laughter was warm and deep and rich.

Tracey Grant

Fathers

My Father

Only recently have I begun to think of my parents as normal human beings. I am still shocked whenever either of them mentions their lives before I was born. I just can't quite believe that they were once my age and that now they have three children. I have started to realise that people do have relationships with their parents and that everyone's is different. It is hard for me to separate myself enough from my relationship with my parents to be able to observe it because I am still so involved but I have chosen to write about my father because I have very strong feelings about him, both good and bad. I am proud of him and don't get embarrassed by him like I do with the rest of my family. I feel that we are closer than a lot of fathers and daughters. We fight a lot, but I think this shows that we care about each other a lot, enough to get upset over things that happen between us.

My dad has always been the more frightening parent. Mum tends to deal with the more trivial things, Dad only steps in when things get serious. I can never stand up to Dad for long. He only has to stick his tongue under his bottom lip for me to start crying. Mum and I tease him about the face he pulls, but only if he is in a good mood; when he does it, it's petrifying. He often gets angry with me if I put myself down or say I can't do something. He says that I am being self-pitying. Sometimes when he is cross or shouts at me I laugh nervously, which makes him even more angry.

When I was younger and wouldn't eat, Dad used to strap me into my high chair and make me stay there until I had finished. Evie, my little sister, was the most fussy child in the world but she never got this treatment. I think that my dad has become soft with old age. In fact, Evie, who is seven, often outdoes him in a willpower contest. Once, on holiday, Evie and Dad sat in a room for over two hours because Evie refused to get dressed and both of them were too stubborn to back down.

His relationship with my brother is less heated but still intense in a different way. Each of us has our special place in the family. I am the oldest, Evie is the youngest and Sean is the only boy. This means that Dad has certain expectations of him although he tries to treat us all equally. Mainly he gets irritated by Sean's lack of aggression. Sean takes after my mum in that he hates fighting and will go out of his way to avoid conflict. This infuriates Dad. I have never seen him so frustrated as when Sean goes into his room to write in his diary, especially if Dad has just told him off.

'Go on, then! Go and mope to your bloody diary!

Go and sulk up in your room and write about how much you hate us!'

On the other hand, Sean probably gets more of Dad's attention than the rest of us. They are forever going to the park to play football or tennis and Sean is the only one of us who can hold any kind of conversation about any kind of sport.

Part of becoming more aware of my relationship with my parents is that I have begun to understand their relationships with their parents. The most interesting and disturbing of these is the relationship between my dad and my grandmother. Dad has a rational approach to most things. I consider him to be very clever and usually trust his judgement unquestioningly. It is because of his level-headedness that it is so terrifying to see him upset, as he is when we go to see Grandma Barbara. It makes me realise that he is only human and that one day I will have to grow up and stop relying on him. Visits to Grandma Barbara are fraught and emotional family occasions and these days I do my best to avoid them. Dad and his mother have never had an easy time together. His mum and dad got a divorce when he was fourteen and since then she has lived alone. This arrangement, despite the fact that she was sometimes miserable, worked all right for a while. However over the last ten years she has been drinking far too much and is no longer independent enough to look after herself.

Because of this tension when we go to see Grandma Barbara, the morning will start with a fight.

'Clare, where's the dog? Evie, have you got your felt tips? How about a tape? Kate, will you come down and help for God's sakes!'

65

Once in the car there will be another argument. Mum navigates and she always wants to turn off on to winding narrow roads as soon as we hit a traffic jam. Dad stubbornly refuses and insists on sitting barely moving on the motorway until the cars trickle forward. As the traffic gets thicker, Dad starts to panic.

'Well, we might as well turn back now.'

'Oh, come on Robbie,' Mum will plead.

'What's the bloody point? By the time we get there she'll be drunk and we'll have to bring her home.'

Unfortunately this is not always far from the truth. There have been many occasions when my grandma has had one too many sherries. One Christmas we arrived to find her on the floor. She was conscious but couldn't remember who we were. It was upsetting enough for me and I hated to think what it must be like to see your mother so helpless. It is on these occasions that I have to look after my dad rather than the other way round and it scares me to be so responsible. I don't like the idea that he is not in control. I would like to believe that he will always take care of me, but times like these make me realise that I will have to take care of myself.

Dad has always had a thing about eating and food is definitely something I associate with him, especially his passion for Amaretti biscuits. He says that in his house when he was younger he and his older brothers would scoff everything as fast as they could because there was never quite enough. I expect that this accounts for his intolerance of fussy eaters. Some of my friends used to be too scared to eat at our house because he was so insistent about us finishing our meals. He treats everyone the same and makes no allowances for guests, which used to embarrass me when I was younger. At the moment he is training to be a child and adolescent psychiatrist and so he deals with a lot of anorexic teenagers. If ever I skip a meal or mention being unhappy with my body, he gets very anxious and expresses this as anger which often leads to rows.

I like my dad best when he is in a jokey mood. He can be very charming and I notice that he is always the centre of attention in a group of his friends. This makes me feel very proud of him. I like the idea that other people are attracted to him. Usually he keeps the conversation going with his slightly dry quips. I can see that he is popular despite the fact that he considers himself unsociable. We have the same sense of humour and he will read me out funny parts of books, or tell me amusing stories about his patients and colleagues. I like it when we go for runs together and he asks me about my friends or school. I feel oddly more comfortable talking to him about private things than I do to my mother. I think this is because he knows how to treat teenagers through his work. He only worries about the important things and I believe him when he encourages me and I trust his advice.

Dad regrets not having done more music as a child. He compensates for this by making sure that we all have the opportunity to learn instruments. Recently he has taught himself to play the accordion and I play my violin with him, which I know he enjoys. I like it too but sometimes I get upset with him if he criticises me.

I used to fret all the time that my parents would

split up because they fight all the time. These days it doesn't bother me because I can see that our family works just as well as any other. My dad doesn't consider himself to be a happy person but his cynical and slightly sarcastic temperament is one of the things I like best about him.

I can see, although he does not boast about it, that he cares a lot about people and is always prepared to stand up for something he thinks important. If there is something that one of his patients needs and is not getting, he will battle it out with the management until they get what he wants for them. He has also stood up for me, against teachers for example. He knows how to be tough when he needs to be and this also makes me proud.

When I blame him for something, he will laugh and say, 'Everyone blames their parents. I'm sure you will spend many happy hours discussing it with your analyst.' He is probably right, but I wouldn't mind passing on the good things to my own children.

Kate Highton

My Changing Relationship with My Father

There are no magic wands in Real Life. My dad has been in prison for several years. Try to get your head round that if you can.

I had an enviably secure life. Mum, Dad, two kids, dog, cat, goldfish. We were the stereotypical nuclear family. Dad and I did a lot of things together. He used to take me to my horseriding lessons every week, his glasses steaming up as he drank his coffee in the driving rain, proudly watching me trot round a field. I remember going flying with him and having to suppress a giggle when he said, 'Romeo Echo Downwind' because it sounded rude, but it made my terrified nerves relax.

While I was growing up, I firmly believed that my parents were omnipotent. They could fix anything, from the school bully to cleaning up cat vomit. But I think everybody reaches an age when they discover that life is unpredictable and can be unfair. When my dad had a near-fatal air crash, it really hit me how much I loved my family. I remember quietly tucking into the chocolates on his hospital beside table, thinking all the time that all we had could so easily have been lost. I think I faced then, for the first time, the possibility of death and the grief of a change you can't go back from.

When Dad was discharged from hospital a month later, he suddenly appeared very vulnerable and, as a result, I took on the protective role in our relationship. The shock of nearly losing him was a great growing experience for me. I think it was at this stage that we reached a more adult phase in our father–daughter relationship. Long after Dad recovered and went back to work, I remained in this protective mode. If he was even a few minutes late coming home, I would panic until he arrived. But I hid this from Dad because I didn't want him to realise how much I worried about him. At times, I wished I was a little kid again, so I didn't have to feel responsible for my dad.

The day my father was arrested is the sharpest memory I have. I remember vividly the outlines of one very tall and one very short policeman seen through the frosted glass of our front door; the WPCs' wide black-and-white ties; the purple ink they used to write down my statement; the shocked, round eyes of my brother when I told him who they were; the policewoman who tried to put a comforting arm around me; my mum making five cups of tea in her best china; and Dad kissing each of us in turn and saying it would all be okay. And all the time I knew that I had to brush my hair or I wouldn't be able to do whatever it was you were meant to do on the morning your father is arrested.

I remember when we first went to see Dad in prison and my first sight of the building they were holding him in: it was built like a monstrous Tescos, all red brick and arches. But all the movies I've watched in my life had not prepared me for what it was like inside, for the way prison doors close, or the smell, or all the bunches of keys. Mum, my brother and I sat on red metal chairs in a room like an airport departure lounge as we waited to see Dad. It was a place where people were used to waiting yet no attempt had been made to make it a human place. Nothing distracted you from your own discomfort and dread.

I stood up when my dad's name was called and walked the twenty steps into a room the size of Wembley Arena. It was full of visitors and prisoners, and behind a table numbered C2 was my father, wearing the red jersey I had given him. After hugging and crying we sat down and tried to act out some vague semblance of normality, talking about everyday things. I really admired Dad for how he tried to make that first visit so much easier for us. He could so easily have sat there crying and telling us how dreadful jail was, how unhappy he felt and how much he missed us. Instead, he tried to cheer us up, entertaining us with funny stories about the other inmates and the officers. He was the same Dad I remembered, always making light of situations, and he made me feel like I could cope, we all would cope.

It was only when we were leaving that my father broke down. He told us he'd be home very soon and that we shouldn't worry. I felt I had to be strong: for him, my mother and brother as well as for myself. But I couldn't. Seeing my parents cry, I felt totally out of control and that frightened me. I just wanted to bury my head under my pillow until the whole horrible situation went away.

In the months leading up to the trial, it actually got easier. I got used to my father being away. Of course I missed him desperately but, as time went on, I adapted to the situation. It felt natural and I expected things to be different between us as we all had so much on our minds with the impending trial. I went from having an ever-present father figure to occasionally seeing someone who did not have the energy to talk about trivial, everyday things. Although these details weren't important compared to the case, they often meant a lot to me. But I coped with this, feeling that if everything went the way they should, things would soon be back to normal between us.

The trial started six weeks before I was due to sit my A Levels. I had started lying to protect my dad, telling him I was working hard so that he wouldn't feel guilty when, in fact, I couldn't be bothered to study at all. This in turn made me feel guilty but I felt I owed it to Dad, who had never let any of his feelings change the way he acted in front of me. I couldn't make him feel worse than he already did.

One day I went to see Dad in court. My father sat in the dock looking so vulnerable in contrast to the police officers who sat around laughing and joking. I felt so angry and confused. At the end of the case, when the verdict went against my dad, I felt stunned, empty. I just couldn't imagine what the future would be like. Until then, I had believed deep down that Dad would be coming home.

It was then I realised that, whenever Dad came home, nothing would ever be the same again. He would have changed, we would have changed and we could never go back to the easy-going relationship we had had before. There would always be this terrible event behind us, an indelible part of our family history.

Dad's now been away from us for something like for ever. I know it's very hard for him to accept how much I've changed. I was still at school when he was arrested, and he must find it difficult to come to terms with the fact that my life is now totally different. He finds it strange that I go to work every morning, that I earn my own salary and that I live away from Mum and my brother. He worries when I take the car out, when I go out at night, or if I'm not home when he phones. It makes life very difficult for me. I feel more and more as if I have to protect him. I have to watch what I'm saying so I don't upset him. In the past, I never had so many secrets. I've always felt guilty about something or other, but now that's more true than ever before. I constantly feel bad about having fun, laughing and not thinking about him *all* the time like I did at first.

Moving away from home has really done me a lot of good as I now have more distance from the situation. Because of my close relationship with my father, I was finding it very hard to separate myself from what he was going through. What had happened to him was more than part of me, it was my whole life. When I spoke to people, it was the first thing they associated me with: I was never myself, I was always his daughter.

In the end, it is the trivia that breaks your heart. It's the smallest details, the things I'll never see or hear again. I'll never need to step over him when he's lying on the floor talking on the phone; I'll never watch him set the bathtaps to the perfect temperature with his feet; I'll never laugh at Mum making him sit on newspaper to protect the sofa from his oily jeans; I'll never hear his Sunday afternoon snores.

Then there are the things that catch you unawares in the middle of a day. Things that happen when I've half forgotten that my dad's in prison and that bring home the enormous gaping loss. Like when I go home to stay for a weekend and stumble across Dad's lost socks or old photographs of what we now call 'Before'. Or answer the phone to someone asking to speak to him, and want to shout 'HOW DON'T YOU KNOW?' Or when I see Dad's yellow toothbrush that I always used to mix up with mine and knowing that it no longer matters which toothbrush I use because he's not here to say, 'Hey, my toothbrush's wet!'

To be honest, I don't know how I see the future of our relationship any more. I can only see us becoming more distant. It's impossible to sustain a normal relationship with someone you were once so close to and saw every day when you now only see them once a week in a room full of other people. We can't even argue or show any signs of emotion without everyone looking at us. There's no privacy at all.

The worst thing is that my father's still stuck in the same situation and I've moved on. I wish life could be put on hold until everything is sorted out. I don't want our old relationship to disappear completely. I still ask myself: when he comes home can things ever be the same again? But I'm an adult now, so do I really want the same father-child relationship as before? We've never had the chance to build a real adult relationship, so it's hard to say what we will have.

Although the love between us is still there, my everyday relationship with my father will have to be rebuilt on a totally new foundation. I see myself differently now. I've become a lot tougher and I find it very difficult to trust anyone or get close to them because I think I'll lose them in the end and just get hurt. I'm starting university soon: I'm going to study Law and live in a new city. I've bought a Wonderbra and I paint my toenails in the summer. And then I wonder, how will Dad ever recognise me when sometimes I can hardly recognise myself?

A.J.

Grandmothers

My Grandmother

It's strange but whenever anyone meets my grandma and me they always say that I am the spitting image of her, not just in looks but in manner and personality as well. Grandma is a tall, sturdy and slightly imposing woman who dresses impeccably and I don't see us as looking at all alike. At times, I'm also offended to hear that our personalities resemble each other in any way. But every now and then I can see what people mean. Although it still surprises me that people who barely know us recognise how much we have in common, I think we are similar in some ways. It's just that circumstances have moulded us into very different people.

As lives go, ours could hardly be more opposite. My grandma was brought up in a huge house and estate in Wales, and I have grown up in a terraced house in central London. I've always been very special to Grandma as my father was one of two brothers. I think Grandma would have loved a daughter and I'm the only granddaughter she has. I think it's partly because I'm so special to her that she has very high standards for me – even though they're not standards I keep.

From an early age, I have often gone and stayed with Grandma on my own. I find it easier to relate to her one-on-one as she always becomes flustered when all five of my family are in her house. When this happens, she becomes very rude about my brothers and me, saying that we are lazy about the house and making comments about the way our parents have brought us up. I can't stand it when she does that.

When I'm on my own, I only have to defend myself against the regular attacks she makes on my clothes, my hair and my manners. She calls my DMs 'beetle crushers' and is always saying that my clothes are either too baggy or too short. She also makes a huge palaver of hiding any slightly revealed bra strap. I have my own way of dealing with this. I just stay quiet through gritted teeth, ignore her and rise above it. But if Dad's there, he gets furious with Grandma and that makes it worse.

As well as the way I present myself, Grandma's other main concern is my safety. I don't think she's ever lived in a city as big as London and I've never lived anywhere else. In true city slicker form, nothing scares me more than pitch black nights and complete silence. My grandmother, on the other hand, sleeps with ear plugs and those eye patch things even in the country, and as you can imagine, she never stays with us in London for long.

Not surprisingly, Grandma's never really understood

that the horror stories she hears in her secluded village about little girls and big cities don't reflect what happens to the majority of the seven million people who reside here in London. I remember when I first started secondary school and Grandma came to visit. As soon as she arrived, she cheerily announced that she'd bought a rape alarm for me to carry on my way to school. I was eleven years old and completely confused. To this day, I've never asked Grandma what she thought would happen to me on my journey on the 73 bus to and from school – and to be honest, I don't want to know.

I remember listening quietly to Grandma telling me how to use the alarm and knowing then that I never would. For quite a while I forgot about the alarm completely. But now I sometimes take it with me if I'm going to be out late on my own. As yet, I've never had to use it but sometimes it makes me feel more confident. At the time, though, Grandma just succeeded in making me feel scared about a place I felt I knew and loved.

Whenever I tell Grandma about my life in London, I still find it almost impossible to explain to her how I've survived for fifteen years. Especially how I've survived going to a normal – as I consider it – state school. Whenever we are discussing my education and I refer to my school as the norm, Grandma always puts me right, telling me not to generalise. She genuinely seems to believe that it is the type of exclusive public school that my cousins attend (partly owing to her influence) that is normal.

My dad, who was sent to boarding school when he was seven, argues with Grandma about education constantly. Dad used to be a teacher and he's dedicated to the state system. He doesn't agree with sending children away to board. My grandma has practically accused him of making things up about his experiences at school. I guess she feels bad when Dad says he was unhappy, and she remains convinced that sending him to boarding school was the right thing to do.

Grandma is always shocked that my brothers and I are taught in 'mixed ability' classes and cannot conceive of her grandchildren in school with the type of 'delinquents' she reads about in the paper. I don't quite know who she imagines these 'delinquents' to be and where she believes they should go to school. I suppose she thinks they should just go and 'disrupt' each other somewhere else.

My earliest memory of my grandmother and my education is of her taking me to school when I was about eight and of innocently leading her up to my classroom and then going off to hang up my coat. I turned around just in time to see my grandmother locked in a warm embrace with my teacher, Mrs Monday. I almost fainted on the spot. Mrs Monday was a young woman whose clothes were bright and alternative, *very* unlike those of my grandmother. For a second, I panicked, thinking that they must be distantly related or old friends. My classmates too were frozen to their seats by this show of affection. I have never been so shocked by anything in my life. When I later asked my teacher if they had previously met, she calmly told me that they'd never set eyes on each other before. To this day, I don't understand what possessed them both to greet each other as old friends. I'm sure now that I never will.

The last time I visited my grandmother, a woman about two years older than me came round to her house in floods of tears. She talked to Grandma for about an hour and then left looking much happier. She'd chosen to come to my grandma for a shoulder to cry on. This quite surprised me as I probably wouldn't come crying to Grandma – and to me, she's family. Funnily enough, I'm often the one my friends come to talk to when they need support, but I never thought of my gran in the same way. Things like this make me feel I probably underestimate her.

It's just that whenever I think my grandmother and I are seeing eye to eye on something, she'll come up with some comment that I never thought I'd hear anyone I know say. As you may have guessed by now, Grandma is a Tory voter. She is also unused to people disagreeing with her opinions. (My parents gave up talking politics to her long ago.) The same is true for me – in that my politics are often shared by the people I know – so, in a way, it's enlightening for both of us. Still, I find her views unbelievably frustrating because they're so sheltered and suited only to the needs of people such as herself.

Even though she's spent hardly any time in London, Grandma is convinced that she understands the problems of the city. She also thinks that people who strike or protest are making a fuss just for the sake of it. I still try to explain to her that, surprising though it may seem, people *do* have better things to do than organise a demonstration just to get on her nerves. But the concept of fighting for what you believe in is so lost on her that the conversation usually results in me wanting to throttle her! Her then telling me that she'd *like* to understand but that she's too old now, only makes me want to throttle her more.

Despite everything I've said, my grandmother isn't naïve or stupid, and in some ways, I admire her a great deal. She has a passion for travel, which I think originated when she was young and went away during the war as a Wren. Even after the war, my grandfather continued to be a Major General in the army, so Grandma spent most of her life moving with him from country to country. Although she's now settled in her own house, Grandma still travels abroad on holiday at least once a year and you can find friends of hers in almost every country around the world. When I imagine how I'll live when I am seventy or so, I really hope that I am still travelling independently and meeting people in different countries like she does.

I also know that life has not always been easy for Grandma and that she's come through it really strong. This strength is something I would be proud to have inherited from her. My father's brother was really ill with schizophrenia for ten years before he killed himself. When I think of the most horrific thing that anyone could ever be put through, it's watching their child be that ill and feeling so helpless about doing anything to make them better.

Sometimes I feel guilty for ever moaning about Grandma. But I know that even though I complain about her annoying habits, and her politics seem to me a hundred years too late for the twentieth century, I do love her. I also try to learn from her views and not just discard them. I just have to say, it isn't easy.

Katherine Bethell

Bibi

Bibi, my grandmother, died five years ago, but it seems to me she has only been dead for a year. It was not until I saw her grave that I finally tried to accept she is no longer alive. Up until that day, I always held on to an image of her 'over there' in Bangladesh, wandering from room to room in the village house where she lived, her sari wrapped around her in the way that old women there wear them so they have no beginning and no end. I would think of her at night, in her silent house with a lamp in her hand, waiting for us to come and visit her again. Now that I look back, I realise I wanted to picture her as lonely because that would mean she needed us. I tried to forget she had many more grandchildren in Bangladesh.

I only knew Bibi for five months. I met and got to know her when I was eight and my family went to live in Bangladesh for a short time. But like a new-found friend you feel you have known for a lifetime, I immediately felt as though I'd known Bibi for ever. She was a friend. In many ways, she was our saviour.

Our parents did not intend our stay in Bangladesh to be simply a long holiday. We were expected to attend Arabic classes during the morning, and Bengali classes in the evening. How we hated those evening lessons and struggled to remain awake over our books! Unlike other adults who would ignore our resentment, saying the lessons were for our own good, Bibi would find ways of saving us from them.

'Halana, Raha, Shaheena!' she would call out in Bengali, 'Come in, it's time for your supper.'

This call would come almost an hour before the lessons were scheduled to end. I knew I must have felt relief when I heard this call, but what I remember most is looking out to the veranda of the house where my grandma would be calling from. She would be slightly bent from the strain of age and looking around as if she was searching for us. By this time, it would be dark outside, but the lamp in her hand would make her dark brown skin glow golden.

The attic was her favourite place in the house, and mine also. It was I who worried about her as she climbed the long flight of stairs to the top as swiftly as her age would allow. I would make sure I was not far behind so I could catch her if she fell.

'Why are you so afraid of life?' Bibi once asked me up there in the attic. She had taken my sisters and me to see the neighbour's cat which had just had kittens. Everyone was enchanted by the kittens but I just hated the mother. In an attempt to protect her newborn she had lashed out at Bibi's hand, and I had just managed to pull Bibi away from those frightful claws in time. That's when she turned and asked me that question. What could I say? How could I tell her I wasn't frightened of life but of death in case it took her away from me?

'Can you swim, Bibi?' I asked one day as she took her midday bath in the pond at the back of the house. I would watch, amazed at how women in Bangladesh could take a bath fully clothed and then change into something dry without uncovering an inch of flesh.

'Yes, I can,' Bibi answered me, laughing. She knew my new-found interest in swimming was only because I had just learnt to swim myself.

'Will you swim for me, Bibi?' As soon as I said this I felt guilty. Perhaps my grandmother was too old to swim? I had always believed that Bibi was very strong because she walked barefoot while I had to protect my feet with shoes. But her stooping posture and creased skin frightened me: it made me think she was feeble.

'Oh, Allah,' I prayed desperately in my head, 'Please don't let her drown.' I was suddenly terrified that Bibi would try to swim just to please me and that the exercise would be too much for her. But Bibi glided through the water, hardly making a splash.

Looking back now my fears seem ridiculous. But I was an eight-year-old child with a frightful imagination and, for a long time after that, I carried a heavy guilt in my heart that I had put my gran's life at risk.

It seems strange that at such a young age I thought so much of death, but I did. My fear probably started from the first minute I met Bibi because her words still echo in my head. We had just arrived at my bibi's village and I was in the middle of a huge crowd of villagers and relatives who were greeting each other with hugs and kisses. I felt drunk with fatigue because of the long journey we had made, and suffocated by the hot air, rich with unfamiliar scents. There was a buzz of people talking all at once around me.

I remember Dad introducing us, saying, 'This is your Bibi, Shaheena.'

I looked up at her and she looked down at me. Then she drew my head to her soft bossom in an embrace. The buzzing around me stopped and words started to fall into place.

'Why did you take so long to come and see me?' Bibi was crying. 'Why did you take so long?'

These first words of hers frightened me. I was under the illusion that Bibi's time was running out and she was soon going to die. But I never discussed this fear of mine. I always thought if I ignored it, it would never happen.

I realise you may think from reading this that I did not know my grandmother as well as I think if I could only see her positive points. But how good she was to us! My father would forbid us to eat beetlenut (a popular food chewed after meals in Bangladesh) but my bibi would give us some in secret. She would also secretly collect glass bottles that we could exchange for honeycomb, which my mother would not allow us to eat often enough for our liking.

Sadly, at the age of eighteen, I have forgotten many of the things that happened during my five-month stay with Bibi all those years ago. But I will never forget the nights. Sharing a bed with my two older sisters, I always ended up uncovered by the blanket in the middle of the night and freezing cold. Then I would wake up and quietly creep into my grandmother's bed, and place my cheeks on her chest. She was so soft and made me feel safe — safe from the grabbing hands and evil spirits of the night. I would feel her chest rise and fall as she breathed and hear her heart beat underneath my head. The rhythm would slowly put me to sleep.

I do recall one time when I was angry with my bibi but looking back, I now see how childish I was being. It had rained heavily that night and Bibi woke me up at five o'clock in the morning to pick mangos. I thought it was a crazy thing to do and didn't want to get out of bed. Then Bibi called me a silly child for not realising that other children would take our mangos, which had fallen to the ground because of the rain. I knew I could not protest so I took the umbrella and basket she had ready for me and stormed outdoors.

Our mango tree was just in front of the house and stood next to an old grave, which was where Bibi's mother-in-law was buried. I had always been terrified of that grave. But now, as I picked mangos, half asleep and furious about being the only one sent outdoors, I forgot my fear of the dead. I sneaked back into bed a few minutes later, leaving the umbrella and basket on the veranda, before Bibi could see that I had only collected three mangos.

The grave by the mango tree was no longer an object of fear to me when I went to Bangladesh last year. This is not because I have grown older but because now my bibi lies there. She lies sleeping under a blanket of earth as she told me she would by the next time we travelled to Bangladesh.

'If we cannot come and visit you, you can come and visit us, Bibi,' I had said the day before our return to Britain ten years ago.

'But how can I leave my home?' Bibi had replied.

I learnt when I went back to Bangladesh a second time that Bibi had always been reluctant to leave her home. This is why she was buried just in front of it by the mango tree. But strange as it may seem, even after seeing her grave, my bibi is not dead to me. To this day I still unconsciously think of her as if she is still living 'over there'.

'It is because we didn't see her on a day-to-day basis that she does not seem missing to us,' my sister once told me.

Secretly, I feel glad. Although I would have loved to have been with my bibi more, I do not want to feel her missing from my life. I will always think of her with a lamp in her hand, wearing her sari in the way that gives it no beginning or end, wandering from room to room in the silent village house, waiting for me. Once again, I will try to forget she has many more grandchildren in Bangladesh.

Shaheena Begum Mosabbir

Friends

Dawn

Nearly all the friendships I've ever had with people have been complicated. They have all had strings attached to them, which in the end, eventually tore them apart. My relationship with Dawn is completely different.

We met in the second year of secondary school, through a mutual friend. I'd just had a really big argument with another girl and felt really alone. Dawn spoke to me about it, and helped me calm down. We discovered we had a lot in common, and it seemed natural that we should strike up a good friendship together.

Our friendship has changed a lot from when we first met. We started out by just hanging about together at school. Then we started phoning each other in the evenings, and soon we began meeting up during the weekends and holidays.

93

Dawn was in a different class from me at school, so we basically went around with different groups of people. We used to meet up at break and lunchtime instead. Dawn also hung out with two other girls, but I think as the years went on, three began to get a bit of a crowd!

I think that the fact that Dawn and I were in different classes helped our relationship. If we'd been together all the time at school, as well as phoning each other up and seeing each other at the weekends, we might have grown bored with each other and that could have destroyed our friendship. Instead, over the following years, our friendship just got stronger and stronger.

All the way through, Dawn and I knew that we would always be there for each other. Most people would see this as a major expectation to have, but we didn't see it that way. We were there for each other because we always wanted to be, and because we knew we could always rely on each other for help and support.

Last year, though, our friendship nearly suffered a big setback. Dawn and I had decided to go to different colleges. It seemed that we were moving in completely different directions, and that our friendship would not be strong enough to handle it. For a while, it felt like we were never able to get together as we had done in secondary school. This was mainly because of time clashes: I work part-time and Dawn always seemed to be busy with something or other.

Even during our college holidays, we were unable to meet up because of all the homework we'd been given as well as my work. We still spoke to each other on the phone, but I felt very bitter towards Dawn because I felt she was totally forgetting about our friendship and going off with her new college friends. She probably felt exactly the same way about me, although we never spoke about it. I guess we were both afraid that what we were thinking could be true, and that our friendship was breaking apart.

In a way I think this was a very important stage for us because, eventually, we both realised that our friendship could change and still survive. It was just moving into another phase. We now have the type of friendship that does not rely on us having to meet up so often. We may not get together for something like six months, but we will often end up speaking to each other for over two hours on the phone about absolutely nothing. So now we run up huge phone bills together instead, which really annoys our parents.

Dawn is still always there to listen to me and help me solve any problems I may have. She is still the first person I turn to in a crisis. Dawn keeps me sane by calming me down about a major exam that is coming up or making me feel better about a huge row I've just had with my parents. I am Dawn's 'agony aunt' too. She comes to me with all her problems, and I always try to give her the best advice I can. She will often tell me later that her mum has given her exactly the same advice as I did. I know Dawn so well that I can instantly tell if there is anything the matter, just by the way she says 'hello' on the phone.

I think I will always have my friendship with Dawn. We will still always be there for each other, and I think we would both be lost if one of us wasn't. I think Dawn and I will end up doing different things in different places, but that we will always write or phone each other and give each other advice. I can't see us ever going back to the type of friendship we had in second-ary school, but I do think our friendship will continue to grow stronger as we get older.

Joanna Hale

What Friends?

Sometimes my friends really get on my nerves. What do you think I should do? Here's the story.

I hang around with eight other girls: Jen, Donna, Jackie, Ann, May, Toni, Lisa and Glenda. We all got together in the first year. Originally we were all in little groups and then we decided to be best friends in one big group. But let me tell you, don't *ever* try having eight best friends! In the past, we all used to argue sometimes, but not like now. Now that we're in the second year it sometimes feels like things *really* aren't working out!

I'll give you an example of a typical day at school. At the start of this particular day everyone was kind of ignoring each other. I was thinking about how we'd all end up in an argument by about lunchtime (it always happens). Our first lesson that day was R.S. I had to sit next to Lisa, which was annoying. She talks and talks. I mean it would be all right if it was interesting but she talks a lot of rubbish. She always tries to impress people, but it never works.

Sitting diagonally opposite me was Glenda. She always falls out with me, or I with her. First of all, Glenda used to hang around with us, me and Lisa. But then she went off with Toni. I don't know what she said to Toni but before you knew it Toni wasn't talking to Lisa and me and we weren't talking to Toni. Then Glenda came back to us. By this time, Lisa and I were friends with Jen, Jackie and Ann. *Now* Glenda keeps going off with Jackie and Ann. That makes Lisa, Jen and me feel cross – the big-headed show-offs!

Of all our group, Jen is really nice. She listens and understands me. I suppose she's my proper friend, and I don't fall out with her much. Donna is also one of my closest friends. But she prefers hanging around with older people, so I hardly see her outside lessons. Jackie is really funny. She's nice, although she does show off. She's slim and quite pretty, but she ain't all that. And she's done everything you can think of with her one million so-called boyfriends.

Ann is a sheep. She copies everything Jackie does and doesn't have a mind of her own. May doesn't say much. She and Toni just go off whispering their secrets to each other.

But on with the story. Right! We were in our first lesson and, unusually for them, Lisa and Glenda were being really quiet. I asked Lisa what was wrong, but she said nothing. Later on, at break time, Jen told me that Glenda had told her that Jackie had had sex with her boyfriend behind the church. Everyone knew except me! I was so annoyed. But as soon as I heard this I thought, Jackie may be rebellious but she's not that stupid. I was angry with Glenda for what she'd said. Everyone agreed with me, and we all immediately broke up with Glenda.

A few days later, we decided to confront Glenda and demand an explanation. But Glenda just burst into tears. She always cries when she wants to get out of things like this. It didn't work.

A few weeks later though, Jackie and Ann made up with Glenda. Then Jackie fell out with me because she thought I'd been mean to Glenda. I was so furious, I had a go at Glenda about it, and she went off crying to Jackie. After days of talking to Jackie, she finally made up with me.

After this, we all decided to give up on the argument. We also decided that we would all make an effort to cause less arguments and try to get on with each other. This worked for a few weeks – until the exams started.

For a whole week before the exams, nobody would stop talking about them, apart from me. (I don't like exams, they freak me out!) Lisa especially wouldn't stop bragging about how her mum and dad had forced her to start revising two months before exam week, so she was expecting to just swim through them. Lisa thinks she knows everything. I must admit, Lisa *does* know some things but the things she knows ain't gonna help her in later life – like all the words for a Jungle tune which nobody else has even heard of.

(My method for exams is to take notes on each subject and then about two days before the exam, read through them and get everything in my head. I do it this way because I find if I start revising weeks before the exam, I end up forgetting it all. I need things fresh in my head.)

Anyway, that whole week I bit my tongue. I decided to let everyone just continue talking about exams. I knew that sooner or later, they'd all get sick and tired of hearing the word, 'EXAM'.

The first day of exam week, before I arrived at school, I felt confident. But I knew that the minute I walked through those school gates, I'd immediately become a nervous wreck. I walked into school and Jen immediately ran up to me. All she could say was, 'Have you revised properly? I'm so scared, I bet I won't even finish the paper!'

I just smiled, but I thought, 'Yeah, and hello to you too!'

Jen just wouldn't stop talking about the exams. In the end, I didn't have any more patience to spare her, so I said, 'Look, Jen, I'm nervous enough as it is. I don't need you making it worse, okay?'

Finally she got the message.

Everyone was in the form room, and all I could hear was more chat, chat, chat, about exams. I thought, 'Lord, help me to keep cool through all of this!'

I went and sat in my seat. Our first exam was Maths for one and a half hours. I knew it was gonna be hard!

The bell went and our exams started. Our form teacher, Mr Morgan, had just gone through all the rules: no talking, no eye contact, no fidgeting, and generally, no noise. When he said, 'Stop, pens down,' we all had to stop whatever we were doing.

Time flew. There were about fifteen questions, and when we were told to stop, I still had another three or four to do. I was disappointed but I didn't let it bother me. I yawned and stretched my arms and looked around. I looked at Jen first, then at Lisa who was sitting opposite her. To my surprise, Lisa was still blatantly writing even though Mr Morgan had told us to stop.

I just turned my face from her and started packing away my stationery. When all our papers had been collected, and we were allowed to talk, Jen immediately said to Lisa, 'You cheated!' Then they both started to argue. By the time we were allowed to leave the room, Lisa and Jen weren't talking, and Jen was off to tell our head of year.

Our head of year said he would consult Lisa's Maths teacher and that we should all go and see him at lunchtime. By the time lunch came round, everyone had sided. Jackie, Ann and Glenda were for Lisa, and Donna was for Jen. May and Toni had decided to keep out. Then there was me. I knew Lisa had cheated, but I just left it. I really couldn't be bothered.

Anyway, we all had to go and see Mr Hendrex, Lisa's Maths teacher. He told us we should forget about it as they'd been through the papers and found no evidence of cheating. I thought for a minute and said, 'Sir, if Lisa carried on writing after the limited time, you're not going to find evidence of that from glimpsing through the papers are you?' Then Mr Hendrex said, 'I'm not really classing that as cheating, so just forget about it.'

We all left the room and while we were walking through the corridor, Lisa said, 'You still think I cheated, don't you?' I told her the truth, and said that I'd seen her carry on writing after we'd been told to

101

stop. Lisa then said that the teacher had told us to finish off all our sentences – which he hadn't – so I just said, okay then, let's just forget about it.

But days later, everyone was *still* arguing and one lunchtime, Lisa nearly hit Jen. Then Lisa started crying, and both Lisa and Jen threatened to leave the school. I told them not to be stupid, their parents wouldn't let them do it anyway. But in my heart, I was so fed up, I thought, 'Go ahead! See if I care.'

In the end we got everything sorted out. We always do. Now we are all friends again – until the next argument that is.

I guess having best friends just isn't easy. The eight main things which I think are essential, and which have helped me through the tough patches are: Love, Peace (if possible), Long-suffering patience, Kindness, Goodness, Faithfulness, Gentleness and Self-control.

These are the main points I think a good friend should have. Of course, these qualities don't make all the anger and cruel thoughts disappear, but they do make life easier. As you've probably discovered, my friends and I aren't what you'd call 'perfect friends'. But I know that in all my friendships, I'm working on achieving all eight!

Charlene Okwei-Nortey

I Want to Be Her Equal

It's difficult to remember a time when I didn't know Lucy. Even though I've only known her for two years, it seems as if she's always been there. In the same way, I don't think I'll ever be able to forget her.

The first time I saw Lucy was at a Welcome Party for the new first years of the school we would both be attending after the summer. The fact that she had enough confidence to ask me my name and where I lived was a marvel to me because I was terrified and so far had barely managed a smile. I was immediately flattered that Lucy had an interest in me. She seemed totally at ease and very much in control, while I was desperately nervous. To me, Lucy stood out more than anyone else at the party.

During the holidays before we started at the new school, Lucy's mum rang up and invited me to her house. I was very scared that I wasn't going to know what to say when I got there, and that Lucy would think I was stupid. When she asked me a question, like how I felt about going to secondary school, I didn't want to give a simple boring answer or just say okay like I usually did.

Even though I was nervous about visiting Lucy, the minute we started talking, I found I could tell her anything and everything about how I felt. In fact, I felt confident enough to practically tell her my whole life story. I'd never felt this comfortable with someone I didn't know before, but with Lucy I felt I could say whatever came into my mind without seeming a fool. I think this was because I felt so relaxed and at ease with her. Lucy laughed a lot at any funny incident that happened or any jokes I told. She was also very funny herself and I immediately warmed to her charm.

I can't remember how we developed into being such good friends after that, we just did. Something had clicked and it was as if we'd known each other for a thousand years. The sense of confidence Lucy gave me was new to me and I liked it. I felt I could explore a part of me I had never really touched before, and this attracted me to Lucy.

I don't know whether Lucy is as confident inside, but outwardly she is very confident. She is very lively and is never dull or boring. She always has energy. She's also very pretty, with a glowing face and a mass of curly blond hair and twinkling blue eyes. Although she never boasts, all this gives Lucy a charm that can attract thousands.

I really like Lucy's wonderful spirit and the fact that she is always a challenge. Because she is so strong, it gives me the spirit to want to be strong too. Lucy wants to be in the army when she is older, but I feel that she is more interested in the assault course than in the actual fighting. I, like Lucy, have a great love for the outdoors and sport, although I envy the energy she has.

There are many similarities between Lucy and me which help us to be friends. Our backgrounds are very similar: neither of us is very rich but we're not poor either. Our parents' beliefs are similar, and our minds link also in the way we feel about certain issues. Lucy is clever like me, so intelligence-wise we have a lot in common. This can cause competitiveness between us. Lucy sometimes calls me a swot but she's just as much of a swot as I am.

Lucy does have weaknesses and I like her for these just as much as I like her for her confidence and spirit. Lucy can get hurt, just like everyone else. She can be scared of doing new things or facing things she'd rather not, like exams. Because Lucy and I are clever, it's important to us to have high marks. Before our summer exams this year, we were both scared but we were able to help each other and calm each other down.

Lucy is very obsessed with being cool and worries about her reputation much more than I do. A word she uses a lot is 'sad'. This usually means people think things that to us are stupid and pointless and do things which to us are totally ridiculous. 'Sad' is the opposite of 'cool'. One year our class play, in which we both played leading roles, won a competition. However, Lucy would not cheer when the news was announced because there were seniors behind us and she didn't want to seem 'sad'.

As much as I like Lucy, it can anger and irritate me that she is so obsessed with her reputation. Sometimes it doesn't matter what other people think. What matters is what *you* think and what *you* want. Lucy loves to get other people's attention and is a great storyteller. But she often exaggerates about things that have happened to her in order to have complete control over her audience. It can irritate me that she will not be honest. It seems she puts on a mask which is really funny, energetic and popular, but sometimes I wish she would just take off the mask and say what she really feels.

It's also impossible to argue with Lucy. If you're unhappy with something she's done, she turns it round so you seem in the wrong for saying anything. Other times, she'll try to turn it into a joke and you just can't help laughing. One time, Lucy promised me that we'd sit together in our new tutorial group. But when the time came, she decided to sit next to Rachel instead, leaving me with no one and feeling hurt at being left out. However, when I told Lucy that she'd said she would sit next to me, she tried to get out of it by joking that she was such an awful person, I wouldn't want to sit next to her anyway.

'Well actually, funnily enough, I *do* want to sit next to you,' I said, still angry.

'Trust me, you don't!' Lucy said, still joking.

At this point, I turned and began to walk away, hurt that she was fobbing me off in this way. As I walked off, I heard Lucy say to Rachel. 'God, she's in a bad mood. She's so over-sensitive.'

Over-sensitive is something Lucy often calls me. But

if Lucy is unhappy with something *I've* done, she will say so and get angry with me.

I feel that I *am* a bit more sensitive to others than Lucy though. When one of my friends was upset about the way someone had been treating her, I spent a long time talking to her and comforting her. Lucy will comfort someone a bit but then find something more important to do. I don't attract people like Lucy does, but I do have many friends who I think are thankful for the fact that I care a lot for them and am sensitive to the way they feel.

The main problem for me is that Lucy is so popular. She gets on so well with everyone and everyone loves her. The same charm that attracts me to her, attracts everyone else. There are people who like Lucy a lot, who I really like as well. But they like Lucy much more than me. I have a friend called Chloe who I've been nice to and friends with throughout the year. Lucy hasn't been friends with Chloe, but because she is so much more popular and a more powerful person to be friends with, whenever Lucy calls, Chloe drops me. Sometimes I worry that people class me as 'sad' and Lucy as 'cool'.

Sometimes Lucy's popularity makes me feel jealous. Lots of people in our class are friends with a group of boys from another school. I had met these boys before and I really liked them and would have loved to have become friends with them, but Lucy got there first. She has become really good friends with them and they all really like her, while none of them even know who I am.

I guess I'm sometimes jealous of the fact that Lucy has everything in life she could possibly want. I can also be jealous of people who Lucy likes a lot. This is particularly true with Rachel. Rachel is also quite popular and play's 'hard to get' when it comes to Lucy. But Lucy really wants to be friends with Rachel and every time she calls, it seems that Lucy drops me and goes straight to her. I feel like someone Lucy knows she will always have, so she needn't bother very much about. But I want to feel special too.

This jealousy also occurs with a girl named Sarah, a friend of Lucy's from outside school. I find it difficult to take that Lucy likes Sarah as much as me and probably more, and that Lucy has lots of fun with Sarah. It's not that I want to keep Lucy to myself, but I do want to feel important in her life.

Most of all, though, I feel that there is a lack of equality in our relationship, and that Lucy always comes out on top. At the moment, I feel as though I have developed out of Lucy because she's such a strong character and we are so close. But I want to be Lucy's equal. I want to be her equal for being myself, Rosie, for having characteristics that people like in *me*. Not to feel that people like me because I am similar to Lucy.

Though it's brilliant being Lucy's friend it's also very difficult. She's so good at everything that I often feel overpowered and think that she's superior to me. It seems that she's got everything and is perfect in every way. She's intelligent and good at all sports. She's beautiful and looks amazing in everything she wears. She's powerful and confident, and gets on well with everyone. I seem so little next to her, there is so much that she's good at and so many ways in which she is better than me.

I think there is a problem in my relationship with Lucy and that is that our relationship isn't clear or fresh. What I mean by this is that when any difficulties arise in our relationship, we don't confront each other and come out with how we feel. So the problems stay there like dust building up on an old book. To brush off the dust and clean out our relationship, it would be good in some ways if we had an argument or a talk where what we felt could all come out.

I don't know exactly how Lucy feels about me. People say that Lucy probably feels the same way about me as I do about her. But I don't believe this because Lucy knows that she's much more popular than me. There's definitely a competitiveness between us that is two-sided and recently at a sports event, Lucy was upset when everyone cheered for me. It would be nice to know that Lucy isn't quite as confident as she seems, because if she was she'd be a marvel of nature!

Despite the complications in our relationship, Lucy and I are best friends. I love having Lucy as a friend and she has said that she likes having me as a friend. The fact that Lucy has weaknesses helps me to be her friend, and our similarities bring us together. Everyone after all has problems, including Lucy, and our relationship wouldn't be so *strong* if she didn't.

Rosie Davis

Amber

Amber and I became close when we went on holiday together to Venice. My father lives there and he'd invited me and a friend to come and visit. Although I didn't know Amber very well at the time, all my closer friends were busy and couldn't come. So I asked Amber if she wanted to go with me. She seemed outgoing and adventurous, and not afraid to have a drink, and that was the kind of personality I wanted to go on holiday with.

Amber and I were in Venice for a week and had a brilliant time. At home, our parents and teachers had been making us both feel claustrophobic; now, for the first time in our lives, we felt completely independent. The holiday was a release from all the pressures of family and school.

The fact that Amber and I were only beginning to get to know each other also made our conversations and activities together more exciting. Both of us were seeing how far either of us dared go – including getting drunk for the first time. I guess you could say that the holiday was our first important bond.

When we returned home, all we could talk about were the things we'd done, people we'd met and places we'd been. Our parents weren't so pleased by our holiday. This was probably because Amber and I came back knowing that we could look after ourselves if we were given more control over our lives – and our parents still felt we were too young.

Over the next year, Amber and I would see each other on and off. We never fell out, we would just go through phases of seeing different people for a while. Then last summer I had some major problems with my mum (as most teenagers do) and I spent a lot of time at a friend's place. I thought we were close but after a very drunken night with Amber, I realised that my other friend didn't really care for me at all. After that, Amber and I started hanging out together. We also started getting into trouble for drinking and bunking off school and our parents declared that we were bad influences on each other. For a while after that, we only got to see each other at school. But we'd always have a lot to say to each other and we were very close.

Throughout our friendship, Amber and I have never lied to each other as we both know that that's how arguments amongst friends usually start. We have always talked things through, and we still do. The only argument I can remember Amber and I having was a few months ago. We were in a history lesson and Amber asked if I could lend her some money for the school shop. I agreed but only if she paid me back straight away. Amber felt she'd lent me so much money over the last year, that I owed her money anyway. Our argument turned quite nasty but I felt I was right so I held my ground – which not many people do with Amber. All our friends were really nervous because they'd never seen us fight before.

At break time after the history lesson, I walked up to Amber in the playground and we talked about it. Amber was still quite heated but it turned out that the real problem between us was that we both felt we were giving more to each other than we got back. We decided to forget all about the money that we'd spent on each other in the past and start with a clean slate from that day on. I think that if any other two friends had the kind of argument Amber and I had that day, they would probably not have talked to each other for a long time to come.

Amber and I are always amazed by how well we know each other. We are so glad we found each other because we share everything: clothes, space, even money. I sometimes think – especially after the argument we had – that perhaps we shouldn't share our money all the time. I know about the quote, 'Never lend a best friend money' – meaning that if you do, you'll never get it back and the trust in your relationship will be gone. Two of my friends went their separate ways after one of them didn't pay the other back a fiver. The girl who didn't pay back the loan had done this before with a lot of things other than money, and her friend felt she was being taken for granted. I can understand how much this hurts and how it can destroy a close relationship. But Amber and I believe that friendship is more important than money so if we feel hurt by each other by accident, we just come out and say it.

Since last summer, I've spent a lot of time at Amber's house. In fact, I'm over there practically every day. We sit and talk over a coffee about who we've seen and what we've done. We watch videos and go out clubbing. We both study Art and I hope to go to art college after school. We've spent whole nights talking about our lives. Amber's told me everything she can remember about herself, from the time she fell off a climbing frame when she was little to her relationship with her younger half-sister who's ill. I think I know her just about as well as anyone can.

I get on with Amber's family too. Her parents don't think I'm a bad influence any more and make me feel like part of the family. I sometimes stay at Amber's house even when she's not there, and the other day, I hung out with her younger brother, Alex. We had a really nice time, watching videos and playing backgammon. In the evening, we did some babysitting together for a friend of his mum's.

From the amount of time Amber and I have spent together, we know we are very compatible. We'd like to get a flat together when we go to college, but we both plan to go travelling for a year first. We have even thought of going back to Venice to visit my dad again, and we always get upset when we have to go on vacation away from each other. We even spent the whole of our work experience together. We were working in different buildings but we'd meet for lunch and then I'd go to Amber's house after work.

If one of us is upset or in trouble, we always drop

everything to help. One morning before work experience, I was flashed at in the park on my way to the office. I was very upset and was allowed to go home. But I preferred to wait until lunch, to see Amber. Recently, the girl I hung around with last summer accused Amber and me of stealing. Our friends all knew we hadn't stolen anything so we didn't really care what she thought. But then, her friend – a boy Amber and I both liked – turned round and accused us of stealing his mate's seventy-pound trainers.

The matter was brought into school and the teacher who interrogated us believed the allegations but couldn't prove them. This upset Amber and me deeply, especially as the boy who accused us was very close to Amber at one point. Now she feels that he can't ever have trusted her because he never even asked whether the rumours about us were true or not. It can get very bitchy at school and Amber and I often just feel like getting out.

In the last few months, I've been a pit paranoid about the way Amber feels about me. I know she cares about me a lot, but sometimes I'm nervous that she wants to meet new people and that I'm holding her back. I don't want to do this, but I find it hard to speak to people for the first time. Amber says she wants to talk to people who can teach her new things. She knows everything I know and this can make me feel as though I want to be more intelligent. Amber has also got herself a boyfriend recently. He's really nice and has made her happier than she has been for quite a while. Still, I'm kind of worried that I won't see her as much as I used to because I know she will have to divide her time between us. But Amber says no man will ever split us up and I believe her.

Another insecurity I have about our relationship is that sometimes I feel like Amber is growing up faster than me. At the moment, I'm trying to act more my age. I'm fifteen, too young to be worrying about the kinds of things I worry about. However, Amber is even more mature for her age, and sometimes I still feel like a child compared to her. But I know that there's still a bit of a child in Amber too.

I think that a lot of my anxiety about our friendship has to do with the fact that we've been too skint to go out much recently. This means that we haven't had much new to talk about. Most of our money is spent on cigarettes. But we've both decided to stop smoking and it's been over a week since my last one. I don't know how well Amber's doing because she is away on holiday with her family at the moment.

It's strange, but when I'm away from Amber I miss her. I think about her nearly all the time. I probably sound besotted by her, and I guess in a way I am. I suppose you would call our relationship quite intense. No one I know is as close to a friend as Amber and I are to each other. At times, we need space apart and sometimes this can cause us to be quite ratty with each other. But because our friendship is so strong, no snapping or argument would ever stop us being friends.

When school begins though, I'll probably see less of Amber because my exams will be starting. I can't say what will happen to us in the future, but Amber and I have promised to keep in touch if we ever get separated somewhere along the line and to meet up again when we are older. I don't know if these promises will come true, but it's a nice idea. Amber and I talk about things like this all the time, along with analysing anything that comes into view. Not many people have conversations like we do.

I guess I'd be a bit lonely if Amber ever left, but I do have other friends and it's a shame I don't see them more often. Still, Amber is the best friend I've ever had and ever hoped to have. She has helped me to be happy with myself and to have more self-confidence in my work and personality. She is also the only person I can talk to knowing that nothing I say will be judged or spread amongst other people as gossip. And I've been the same kind of friend to Amber in return. I hope our friendship lasts a lot longer than most and I'm pretty sure it will.

Jolene Farmer

Boyfriends and Girlfriends

Paul

Paul was one of those people I'd vaguely known for years before anything actually happened between us. When we were younger, we used to hang out in a huge group together. We'd go running through the woods, doing things we weren't supposed to do, like drinking or breaking into boarded-up houses. I'd really liked Paul then but nothing had come of it. Gradually, we'd all drifted into other friendships.

For a while after our gang broke up, Paul stayed on my mind. From time to time, I felt that if given the chance, it would be good to quench an old desire and become more intimate with him – even if only briefly – to satisfy the part of me that had once liked him. But that had been years ago and I'd all but forgotten about him. I'd been involved with other people and he was just someone I'd once hung around with.

Then two Christmases ago, my close friend Josie

decided to throw a party and, out of the blue, Paul and some of his friends phoned her up looking for an invite. (Funny how news of parties travels so fast!) As it was going to be a big party, and knowing that I'd once been interested in Paul, Josie said they were welcome to come.

The party was a huge success – bar one or two scandals. Everyone had a fantastic time whilst consuming far more alcohol than could possibly have been good for them. Eventually Paul and his mates arrived, by which time things were in full swing. I was immediately informed of how great he was looking and, with extra courage provided by the weird and wonderful punch Josie was serving, went over to chat to him. We spent the rest of the evening talking to one another. A friend told me later that you could literally see the sparks crackling between us.

That night we both ended up staying over at Josie's, along with most of the other people at the party. We didn't sleep together, which, looking back, is probably a good thing. If we had, I would doubtlessly have become even more attached to him than I later did.

I had learnt from previous experience not to expect anything to continue after getting together with someone at a party. I had thoroughly enjoyed my evening and, after kissing Paul goodbye in the morning, was just pleased that I'd had so much fun.

What changed my attitude was learning through a mutual friend that Paul had expressed some interest in me after that evening together. (This probably explains why our relationship was destined never to work. From the very beginning, anything to do with the verbal expression of our feelings for one another was done through somebody else. Our lack of communication was a fundamental flaw: we could talk for hours about everything apart from what was going on between us. At the beginning though I wasn't even aware that this might be a problem. I was just flattered to hear that he liked me too.)

For the next couple of months, Paul and I would see each other socially, in a group with our friends. We were together, but we never spoke about how either of us saw our relationship. It became worse the longer it was left. I liked him more and more, so I felt less and less inclined to rock the boat as it were. It was an insecure vicious circle. I wanted to know where I stood, but the stronger my feelings became, the more scared I was that if I started hassling Paul about it, I would push him away.

I found – and still do find – the transition in myself quite amazing. I am normally a person who deplores this kind of behaviour. I think it's dreadful just to accept whatever is offered in a relationship, never questioning the way a man treats you and suppressing your own wants for fear of losing him. Yet here I was behaving exactly this way myself.

I would ring Paul up and have a conversation which was comprised entirely of me babbling away and him barely grunting in acknowledgement. By the time these phone calls ended, I would be cringing at myself. Once, at the end of an evening, when Paul and his mates were leaving and we were saying goodbye, I said to him, 'Look, we should sort this out.'

'Fine,' he replied, 'But not now, I have to go.'

Then he kissed me and left.

The worst part of it was that I was over the moon. Paul had said we could sort this out!

Eventually, I got sick of making a fool out of myself, and I stopped ringing him. The problem was that I still had very strong feelings for him. I was immensely attracted to him physically, but also I missed the conversations we had had. I knew that there were major problems on the expressing-our-feelings front, but I couldn't help the way I felt. At least when we had been together – a term I use loosely! – I had been happier (though more insecure). Now I was just miserable, sitting and thinking about him all the time. The more people told me how much better off I was without him, the greater the loss I felt.

A month went by without Paul and me seeing each other. But I was still completely infatuated by him. Alex, the same mutual friend who had originally told me that Paul was interested in me in the first place, now told me that Paul was asking after me and still really liked me. Alex said that if I still liked Paul then I should call him up, because he was definitely still interested in me. If only Paul could have told me that himself!

In the end, of course, I called. And from our first telephone conversation, things seemed infinitely better. Paul was chatty, friendly and made much more effort than he'd ever done before. We began seeing a lot of each other. I was so happy that I'd swallowed my pride and phoned because things were going so well. We both talked a lot and covered everything from politics to each other's families. But good as all this was, there was still no discussion about where either of us saw the relationship going. No boundaries were ever established. Although it was obvious we liked one another a great deal, and we expressed this physically, I never knew if Paul saw what we had as a serious relationship or as just a fling.

Looking back, I think I overcompensated for this aspect of our relationship by trying too hard. I think I must have intimidated Paul quite a lot – I'm a year older than him and very opinionated – although at the time, I didn't see this because I was trying so hard to be what I thought he wanted me to be. I couldn't possibly have known what this was as Paul probably didn't know himself. Perhaps neither of us was mature enough to express how we felt towards each other for fear of being laughed at or rejected.

I believe that people pick up signals subconsciously, so, while I was desperately hoping that things would work out between Paul and me, and trying hard to make him like me, he subconsciously (or otherwise) knew that he could do whatever he wanted and it would be okay. At times, I felt that we were really getting to know each other. At other times, I didn't even recognise the person I was when I was with him.

This was why I felt so cheated when I went away for a weekend and Paul got together with somebody else. He didn't know me at all, so how could he leave me? I was told by several different people how much he had liked me, but this just made me feel worse. If we'd been able to talk about our feelings, maybe things would have been different. Instead, everything had been based on guessing games which had made me act completely out of character.

I am not by nature a jealous person, so my reaction to Cathy, Paul's new girlfriend, astonished me. I'd never met her, but I hated her. Even now, months later, though I feel no animosity to Paul any more, the mention of Cathy's name still brings a vague sneer to my face. I think this has less to do with Cathy – after all I don't know what she's like – than how Paul's action made me feel about myself.

Initially though, by disliking the person Paul was with (even though I never saw her) I could pretend to myself that the break-up in our relationship was her doing and not his. Of course, this didn't make me feel any better. Especially when Paul called round to collect a tape he'd lent me, and could barely look me in the eye. In the end, he rushed off, mumbling some excuse about his mother waiting outside in the car for him. I was absolutely furious! For several weeks I went through the complete range of misery and self-loathing, as well as raging at Paul and embarking on huge bouts of 'Where did I go wrong?'. All these feelings seemed to be mixed up together, forming one huge swelling of emotion somewhere between my head, my heart and my belly.

Even after these feelings eventually died down, it still took a very long time to get over Paul. This was partly because I never seemed to meet anyone I liked anywhere near as much as I'd liked him, however much he had hurt me. What I couldn't explain to people once I really *was* over him though was that, in spite of everything, I still wanted us to be friends. People found this ludicrous, but it was true. I really wanted to be able to ring Paul up, or meet him, and for the side of us that had been friends to remain friends. We had got on so well together and we shared a similar sense of humour. There was also a feeling of wanting some acknowledgement that I'd meant more to him than another notch on the bedpost, or another face amongst many.

I was lucky enough to finally receive this acknowledgement about a year after we'd split up. By this time I was well and truly over Paul! We didn't see each other much, as we move in completely different social circles, but once again we'd both ended up at the same party. We saw each other at the same time, but seemed to mutually agree not to recognise that the other person was there. (Old habits die hard!) The party was terrible and I was already going through some other trauma at the time. All of which helped me decide that the evening couldn't get much worse, so I went over to speak to Paul.

In the end, that move just about made my night. We had a really nice chat. We were both genuinely interested in what each other was doing, and he actually brought up some of our old private jokes. This suggested to me that I had meant something to him, something that differentiated our time together from our time with other people. I felt as though a chapter in my life had finally been closed the way it should have been.

When I think about Paul now, I remember him fondly. Although he hurt me a lot at the time, I think it was a character-building experience! I wouldn't change that experience because it has helped me form much healthier, more communicative relationships since. I would never belittle a relationship like this, even though I am over it now, because I think that every relationship teaches you a little more about yourself.

Jessica Shaw

Alison

After I realised I was gay, I found that my main problem was identifying other lesbians. I saw many other women I was attracted to, but I could never make myself ask them out in case they weren't gay. I had no gay friends and wasn't old enough to go to gay bars. I was completely alone – or at least I thought so at the time.

I had known Alison through college before I met her socially. I would never have thought Alison was a lesbian. Alison is more subtle in her appearance – not like me with my shaved head and nose ring. If I hadn't found out from someone else that she was gay, I would never have flirted with her.

One evening, my sister, Louise, and her friends invited me out for a drink. The atmosphere at the pub that night was full of life. It was packed and there were people singing old-times songs on the karaoke. We all got our drinks and found a table near the door. Soon after, my sister's friend, Dave, was asked to dance by a woman at least four times his age and he immediately disappeared off into the crowd. Then I spotted Alison and asked her to join us.

I'll never forget that evening. I was very open and loud, playing up to my new lesbian friend. Not much conversation took place, but the flashing lights of the disco and the laughing voices around me made a great atmosphere. It was raining hard outside and that made the pub seem even more jolly. I remember leaning over and nibbling at Alison's peanuts after she told me how she hated all the salt. The two of us were huddled up in the corner. I was thrilled by how comfortable Alison was with me. She was being very loud and flirtatious too. Although I wasn't aware of it at the time, Alison also knew I was gay, which is why we'd connected so easily – unlike my earlier attempts with other girls.

All of us at the pub that night were very energetic, dancing around with the rest of the crowd. Then we decided to go to another pub fives minutes down the road. I remember Louise, Alison and Dave running down the road ahead of me, singing in the rain as I walked slowly behind. The walk and the rain on my face started to sober me up. All I could think about was Alison. I knew I liked her, and I felt that she liked me too. Then I snapped out of my thoughts and raced to catch the others up. We entered the pub to the sound of 'Baggy Trousers' by Madness – my favourite group and my favourite song.

I don't know why, but in this second pub, I suddenly felt shy and a little out of place. We hadn't been sitting down very long when an old man came over to talk to us. I couldn't really understand what he was saying (perhaps because I was still a little drunk) but I talked to him anyway. During the conversation, I felt a tingle all over. Alison had put her arm behind me and was stroking my back. This continued for five minutes until finally, I turned round to face her and asked her to stop. But she just leant her head on my back and pretended to get involved in the conversation.

Later, when I was in the toilets, I turned round from washing my hands in the sink to find Alison standing in front of me. We didn't say anything, but we had our first kiss.

The first month of our relationship was pretty much the same as any relationship, gay or straight. We spent most of our time alone together, at each other's houses, at the cinema or out walking. We were getting to know each other's minds, our likes and dislikes.

I'd already got over the initial stage of coming out as a lesbian — or so I thought. But the truth was that telling everyone I was gay had been relatively easy. Actually leading that lifestyle, and being seen in a lesbian relationship, proved a much harder experience.

My mum had been okay when I'd come out to her two years before but she'd never actually asked anything about my sexuality until I met Alison. Then, a couple of months after Al and I had been going out, Mum turned to me while we were watching TV together, and out of the blue asked, 'Are you and Alison friends or "Let's Be Friends"?' This was her subtle way of asking whether Alison and I were having a relationship, and I told her that we were *Good Friends*. There was a sudden silence in the room so I asked Mum if she minded. She told me quite bluntly, 'If you don't mind my boyfriend, I don't mind your girlfriend.'

I guess everything's pretty much straightforward in my household. But although everyone says that my sexuality's okay that doesn't mean it's always liked. When I first came out to my family, I felt they didn't give me much support. And when I met Alison, I still didn't feel I had their support. I didn't feel comfortable having my family or my friends around me when I was with Alison because they tended to see her as a 'fact', as evidence of my sexuality.

Up to then, most of the friends that I'd hung round with had accepted my sexuality, and the boys had just behaved as if I was one of the lads. By the time I met Alison, most of my friends were already in relationships. We'd all meet up to go to parties or the cinema, but there was still a sense of discomfort when Al and I were around.

Alison had never spoken to her family about her sexuality, and for a long time after we started going out, we were seen by them as just best friends. This put a lot of pressure on our relationship as I felt I wasn't being honest with her family. Eventually, Alison came out to her mum and told her about me. Her mum likes me a lot, but our relationship's still not talked about.

It was a strange feeling at first to love Alison. It had taken me a long time to admit to myself what I really wanted: I'd denied my sexuality for years before I came out and had been prepared to settle for part of a life. But despite the difficulties, being with Al made me feel more at ease with myself because, for the first time, I was able to know that it really did feel right.

We spent most of our first summer together cycling. Then we went back to college. We weren't able to be out at school and this created problems in our relationship. Because Alison had just started her A Levels and I was in my final year, we were in separate classes and only saw each other during breaks. I was always pleased to see Alison, but we both felt we behaved unnaturally. We weren't able to talk to each other the way we did when we were at home. We were best friends at school and a couple in private. We were living a double life and it felt like more denial.

I began to feel more and more claustrophobic, as if I was suffocating. We were in the closet at school, and my friends and family never encouraged us to be open about our sexuality either. One night, my brother had all our friends round to the house. We were all sitting in his room, talking and being friendly. Then my brother, who'd gone off for something, walked in and saw me giving Al a kiss. He immediately asked me to leave the room. I felt really betrayed, and lonely all over again.

Throughout the school year, things went on in much the same way. Alison and I argued a lot, and ended up blaming each other for our feelings of isolation and hurt. I've always felt that although Alison and I are in a lesbian relationship, our communication problems are much the same as those in any straight relationship. It's just society and people's attitudes that make it different and more difficult. But, despite our problems, Alison still helped me through my second year of A Levels by giving me confidence and love.

Last summer, after Al and I had been together a year, we decided to go to Lesbian and Gay Pride. (I've never got into the gay scene much, because gay clubs and bars have never really appealed. Socially I'm a very quiet person, so Alison and I have led a pretty 'straight' lifestyle, going to our local pub and cinema.) I can still remember the shock I felt when I arrived and saw so many lesbians and gay men openly having a great time. I was shy at first, but was able to get enough confidence after a while to start to show my love for Alison publicly. It was fantastic to be able to put my arms around her and kiss her.

For most of that day, I just lay on the grass with Alison and soaked up the atmosphere. At one point, Alison got very upset. I asked her what was wrong but she wouldn't tell me at first. Then she said, 'I'm crying because I'm happy.'

'Well that's good, isn't it?' I replied. I suppose after the pressures of dealing with our families and keeping our relationship a secret at college, Pride was a day of freedom. But Alison was crying because she felt we only had one day out of a year to be proud.

Things have changed a lot in the last half a year since then. Alison has moved in with me and my family and we share a room. Mum is always giving us little presents and things which make us both feel accepted. My brother and sister both love me and Alison very much, and all of Alison's family like me a lot too. So things have become a bit easier for us. I've left college now and am going on to do a foundation course, and Alison is sitting her last year of A Levels.

I still haven't got into the gay scene, but Alison and I are now a lot more open about being a couple wherever we may be. It took us a year and a half, though, to feel good about our relationship. To feel it wasn't weird or abnormal. A year and a half to feel accepted. I still have my fears of the future and of the problems that may still arise from being gay, but the last eighteen months have proved to me that I have a strong will to be happy.

Sometimes, when I notice how similar my body is to Alison's I think it's strange that our relationship feels this good. But I guess every lesbian must think that.

Liz Pike

Michael

Looking back, I wonder if I could have avoided the terrible situation I found myself in. Then again, how could I have known?

I was never attracted to Michael. But everyone else in the school liked him, and that was important to me. Actually, they were all probably afraid of him. He was the strongest person in the school and he had a violent temper. So it's not surprising that everyone did what he wanted. At the time, though, I thought Michael was popular and I wanted him to notice me.

I finally succeeded when we went on a school trip to Brighton. I was wearing a black ripped tee shirt with a red belly top and leggings. I was the first person in school to wear this new look, and I was aware of the other girls watching me. I always did love attention.

On the coach, Michael sat next to Katrina and

Marshime who were well known to be 'loose girls'. Everyone said they enjoyed sleeping with lots of guys. I had no idea if this was true but that was the reputation they had. Getting a 'bad' name guaranteed that everyone at school would gossip about you. Much as I liked to be noticed, that was not the kind of attention I wanted. Most of the girls Michael hung round with had this reputation and, watching Katrina and Marshime, I hoped I would never get labelled that way.

It wasn't until we were on our way home that I realised Michael was interested in me. On the coach back, he sat behind me and I could feel him watching me. He even brushed his fingers softly across my neck.

His friend, David, who was sitting next to him, whispered, 'She's not into them kinda things, Michael. Leave her alone.'

I just acted as though I were asleep, not wanting to make a move one way or another. But I was very excited and I wanted something to happen.

The next day during our school lunch break, I convinced my best friend Tara to come with me to watch the boys play football. Michael was in his usual corner, surrounded by his usual gang. I knew he was watching me but I acted as if I couldn't see him and began a conversation with Tara. The boys from our class scored a goal against the other team, and Tara and I began cheering and screaming.

Just then, a boy called 'Little Bobby' tapped me on the shoulder. When I turned towards him, he said, 'Michael wants you.' I wasn't surprised by the message and did as I was told. I just followed Little Bobby to where Michael was standing, leaving Tara by herself.

When we reached Michael, 'Little Bobby' and the

135

other boys immediately walked off, leaving us alone together. It was as if they had planned it. I had never spoken to Michael before, and his first words to me were 'hold this'. I put out my hand and did exactly as he asked.

Michael removed a little orange packet from his back pocket which turned out to be a packet of Rizlas. He took out a couple of small sheets of white paper, licked the edge of one of them, stuck them together and placed the papers in my outstretched hands.

'Stand still,' he said, all the while looking into my eyes.

Then he produced a small clear plastic bag from his pocket, like the kind you get with spare buttons in it when you buy a new dress. In the bag was something that looked like thyme leaves. He sprinkled these on to the sheets of paper in my hand.

'Bobby!' he shouted, and Little Bobby came running over with the end of a cigarette which he gave to Michael before quickly disappearing again. Michael added tobacco to the leaves, then took up the papers and carefully rolled them between his fingers before licking them down in place. He lit the rolled-up cigarette, inhaled deeply with closed eyes, held in his breath for a few seconds, opened his eyes and exhaled in my face. When he saw my confused expression, he laughed, then took my hands and put his arm around my waist. I knew everyone could see.

The next day I had arranged to meet Tara in the school garden at lunchtime. But that morning I was given a message that I should meet Michael in the library, so I went there instead. When I walked into the library, Michael was sitting right at the back with his friend David. He pulled me by the hand to sit on his lap. When I looked at him, I noticed his eyes were red and I knew he'd been smoking again.

'Have you got a boyfriend?' he whispered in my ear with his face slightly touching my neck.

I shook my head.

'What about it then?' Michael said.

David quickly turned to look at me with a worried expression on his face, but he said nothing. I understand what that look meant now.

I had wanted Michael's attention, but going out with him was a different thing altogether. I would have to kiss him – something I really didn't want to do.

'I'll think about it,' I said. 'Don't rush me though, we've got all the time in the world.'

David looked relieved. And Michael didn't press me any further.

For the next few weeks, Michael and I hung round together at school. We'd also see each other a bit after school. We'd sit on the walls near his flats and chat. Things were fine, and Michael didn't pressure me into saying that I was definitely going out with him.

Then, suddenly, everything changed. I was talking to Darren, a good friend of mine from drama class, on my way to a lesson one day. We were having such an interesting conversation, we didn't realise we were the only ones who weren't in our classes yet. We were mucking about, trying to make each other's school ties look better, when Michael came walking down the corridor. The instant he saw us, he started shouting.

'Is that why you don't want to go out with me? Are you dealing with Darren, ha? Answer me!'

Then he grabbed me and began shaking me against

the wall. I couldn't answer him, I was so shocked by his behaviour. Poor Darren tried to get Michael to stop shaking me, but Michael suddenly punched him in the chest, leaving him screaming in pain. Then he dragged me out of the school.

He walked me to his flats and sat on the wall. He smoked a draw and then started crying. I didn't say anything. I knew he didn't want me to speak.

'Don't ever do that again,' he said. 'Don't talk to no man unless I say you can.'

The next day Michael was waiting for me at his flats which were on my way to school. He called me over and made it clear he wanted me to stay with him and David. I didn't want to provoke Michael's temper, so I decided to do as he wanted. By now, I'd grown afraid of Michael and would shake within myself whenever he touched me. We spent the day, sitting on the wall outside Michael's flats, him, myself and David.

At one point, David and I went to buy something to eat with money that Michael had borrowed off me. As we walked to the shops, David said that he was sorry I was mixed up with Michael. He said he would have treated me better. I didn't say anything, I just tried to smile. Only I couldn't.

When I went to school the following day word had got round about Michael and me. Darren wouldn't talk to me. Michael had warned him off, and he wasn't the only one. Most of the boys were behaving strangely towards me. Usually, I'd talk and joke with the boys in my class, now they would hardly even look at me.

That lunchtime I saw Michael eating with David and the gang in the playground. I stormed towards him and raised my voice as high as I possibly could.

'How dare you? You don't own me,' I shouted. 'Who the hell do you think you are?'

I couldn't believe Michael's response. It was as though I was behind a glass door and he couldn't hear a word I was saying. He just carried on joking and chatting with 'the boys'. Finally, when he was ready, he turned around, wiped his mouth with a tissue, said 'Excuse me', and took my hand and led me out the school gates. We walked in silence until we got to the walls outside his flats.

Once there, Michael built another 'draw' and, as usual, exhaled fully into my face. His first words were, 'Haven't you got a coat? I don't like the guys watching you.' I was so angry, I decided to play him at his own game.

'No, I don't and you know what, I enjoy being watched by the guys. It's better than being watched by you.'

It was only when I noticed that everyone around was staring at me and felt the side of my face burning that I realised Michael had slapped me. I began to run away from him, slowly at first, then faster as the tears fell from my eyes. I didn't stop running until I reached David at the school gates. He knew what Michael had done even though neither of us mentioned my face which was burning and marked with the impression of Michael's ring. Not long after, Michael showed up acting as though nothing had happened.

'Why'd you hit her, man?' David immediately asked.

'Just cool,' Michael replied. 'If she was your girl, you'd understand.'

'I ain't nobody's "girl"!' I wanted to shout but I didn't. David and Michael probably wouldn't have heard me anyway. They were too busy arguing about whether Michael was right to treat me the way he did. I couldn't believe it. I had *never* agreed to go out with Michael, and now both he *and* David were acting as though we were.

Then in the middle of their row, David slapped Michael's draw out of his hand. No one else would have dared do that to Michael. I just sat on the floor, my mouth wide open and my hand covering my bruised cheek. By this time, the whole of the fifth year had gathered round us, and everyone in the school yard was watching.

Michael just stared at David in disbelief. He began to shake his head and I could see hatred welling up inside him. But it was all directed at me. Michael couldn't do anything to hurt David and David knew it. They'd been best friends since the age of two.

'I'll get you back,' Michael said to me. 'I'll do something bad to you.' His eyes were blaring red.

He did.

It was the last day of school and I'd stayed behind after everyone had left to help my head of year with some clearing up. By the time I left, the school was deserted. I walked out through the gates and turned towards the alleyway which was a short-cut across the park that led to my house. Then I decided against going through there and turned back. As I swung around, someone grabbed me from behind. He had one arm under my arms and he covered my mouth with his other hand. I knew straight away that it was Michael.

I began kicking him, but someone grabbed my legs. Michael had my arms locked in an awkward position, making it difficult for me to breathe, and there were two other boys with him. I recognised one of them, John, who was one of the most hated characters at the school. He was always in trouble and was also one of the only people who wasn't afraid of Michael. The third boy I didn't know.

I struggled against them for what seemed like ages, biting, scratching, kneeing and head-butting. But there was nothing I could do. They unbuttoned my shirt and touched me, and put their hands up my skirt, whilst holding me down. I had a really nasty time. I was scared I was going to be raped but they stopped short of this and eventually they ran off and left me. I walked back through the park by myself feeling angry, scared and confused. I couldn't tell anybody what had happened.

The next day, Michael phoned me. 'I've got a new girlfriend,' he said.

You never had one in the first place, I thought to myself, and put the phone down. It rang again and I suppose it was him. I didn't pick it up.

Now, I'm left very changed. I am much quieter than I used to be. I am not interested in going out with boys or going to clubs or parties. Since I left the school I haven't seen anyone I used to know there. I no longer enjoy attention and I keep myself to myself most of the time. I feel pessimistic about these changes.

Because of Michael, I drifted apart from my best friend Tara. I'd let her down and our friendship was affected. But in the end, even though I never told her exactly what happened, she began to understand what

Michael had put me through and now we talk on the phone sometimes.

Luckily, we moved flats at the same time that I moved from school to college, so I don't see Michael at all any more. But until very recently, I felt I couldn't tell anyone what Michael did to me – and up to now, I never have.

Melanie Lorene

Fantasy Football(er)

This piece is not about a real relationship. At least not in the conventional sense of the word. But it is about the kind of relationship that often seems the most solid, reliable and real to me. It's about the relationships I have in my head. Fantasy relationships. And, in particular, my unrequited adoration of a certain footballer!

Darren Anderton, at the time of writing, plays for Spurs. Manchester United are reportedly interested in him but the chairman of Spurs has vowed to keep hold of Darren at all costs – and I don't blame him for a minute. Darren plays on the wing, and is one of the few footballers who are playing consistently well for England at the moment. But that's not the whole story. Darren is beautiful – in a sort of gangly, not sure what his limbs are doing at any given moment, kind of way. This is something I can identify with, having lost control of my extremities when I 'shot up' a few years ago. And maybe that's why I love Darren. Because no matter how uncoordinated he may seem most of the time, when he is running down the wing, Darren is the most beautiful sight in the world.

It is also true that I have never seen Darren gob or empty his nose on the pitch. I therefore imagine him to be that rare thing: a gentleman in the sometimes uncouth world of football. Whether this is true or whether cameramen all over the country are simply protecting me from the horrible truth, I cannot say. Darren does, however, have a nice line in swearing explicitly whenever his limbs rebel and put the ball somewhere it shouldn't be. This hasn't tarnished his image for me in the least. Rather I regard it as an attractive weakness – especially, again, as it is one of my own.

My crush on Darren highlights one of the major problems of being a female football fan, though it's an issue rarely acknowledged by the sporting press. The obscene requests that women receive from fellow fans of the opposite sex and the inadequate toilet facilities at stadiums across the country are familiar complaints, but these are nothing compared to the agonies I go through for Darren. I am not a Spurs fan you see. I support Ipswich. And when we played Tottenham last season, I was forced to confront the painfully gorgeous sight of Darren speeding towards our goal with disturbing frequency.

As our defences melted, ran the wrong way, or simply fell over, I felt increasingly faithless. And when I started wanting corners to be given *against* us – Darren takes them for Spurs – I began to feel that the only way out was to leave the grounds and quietly shoot myself for having no morals. I will not, however, have this problem this coming autumn. The sight of various enemy strikers speeding towards our goalposts became so common last season that we have been relegated.

My younger brother finds my crush on Darren horrifying. The idea of one of the pure and holy players of football being reduced to an object of his sister's affection appals him. He has taken to scribbling violently abusive messages over my photos of Darren and delights in showing me pictures in which my hero is looking less than attractive. Recently, however, our sibling relationship has improved somewhat. My brother's newly discovered interest in girls has suggested to him that perhaps I am not as insane as he first thought. As a result, me and my fantasy men are slowly becoming more acceptable. A few weeks ago he even brought me an action photo of Darren which he must have torn from *Shoot* or *Match*. He said nothing, but it was a touching moment.

Darren is simply the most recent addition to what I call my 'little house-by-the-sea club'. This club is made up of the men that if I, Aladdin style, were granted three wishes, I would whisk away to 'a little house by the sea', possibly somewhere near Portsmouth. There, we would all spend the rest of our days together. Actually, my house may have to be an estate because, although mine is an exclusive club, the numbers are growing, and I'm quite sure not everyone would get on.

At last count, my chosen few numbered around twenty, and I'm proud to say that they are an eclectic bunch. Keeping company with Darren are my snooker players, Alan McManus and Ronnie O'Sullivan, an assortment of stand-up comedians, the sacked drummer of Oasis – sacked, obviously, because he was by far the best-looking among them – a couple of actors called Tim (Roth and Robbins) and one of my oldest fantasy companions, Alan Cumming, who has the most radiant smile in the country. This list goes on, and changes constantly.

These then are my constant companions. Women's magazines exhort us to keep our girlfriends as boys come and go. My experience says friends come and go, but imaginary boys are always available when you need them and far away when you don't. My fantasy companions can be relied upon to pop up at the most useful times. One of them is almost invariably around during mind-numbing lessons. Also, the teacher can't berate you for conversations you conduct with them in your head, as obviously, no one can hear them but you.

My fantasy companions always accompany me at times of stress and almost instinctively know exactly what is worrying me at any given moment. This avoids all those tedious heart-to-hearts that we usually have to indulge in to get people to empathise with us. Basically, unreal relationships seem to me infinitely more handy than the real sort. Even arguments and heartbreak are readily available for the more melodramatic – some might say, realistically minded – among us, and satisfying dramas can be made up at will.

At this point I would like to disabuse you of the idea that the membership criteria for my house-by-the-sea club are based solely on physical charm. Some of my men have been selected for pure talent alone.

Many people find this hard to believe – including my mother. At fourteen I remember being outraged by her suggestion that I'd included my favourite speedway rider in the club simply because I fancied him. For a start, I'd never seen him without his crash helmet on. (I could, I suppose, have been taking fantasy relationships to a new extreme: fantasy faces.) But my mother was not convinced.

Most of the time, however, I think my mother enjoys having a teenage obsessive in the house. Sometimes our tastes even coincide. Just the other day we happily watched a film staring Keanu Reeves together, and my appreciative comments were met with nothing but nods of agreement.

I would like to think that embarking on this wonderful kind of relationship was a common trait amongst sensible girls my age. But though my gut feeling says that it is, experience tells me otherwise. It could be that my tastes are dire – but no one wants to tell me – or perhaps the numbers in my club are too big and border on the distasteful. All I know is that the funniest looks I've ever received are when I openly express my adoration for one of my boys.

Close friends *have* got used to hearing the details of my current obsession. They know that if I gush to the point where it gets boring I can be distracted by something amusing in the real world, a funny number plate or something. But further out in my circle of acquaintances, being so open about the men in my life seems to be considered a bit over the top and my confessions are greeted with horrified amazement. Maybe it really is the case that nobody else indulges in these kind of fantasies. Or perhaps it's that the whole subject's taboo, and nobody else has the guts to admit they do it too? It's at times like this I feel I am performing a public service. Sort of 'Hey, folks, you too can be dangerously obsessive and still take part in normal society'. I hope I have helped.

There are problems, of course, with fantasy relationships – as there are with relationships of any kind. Daydreaming, especially when you have twenty different daydreams to choose from, is much more attractive than any sort of work. And you can get a reputation for being a bit strange when your mind wanders in public and you find yourself walking round with a demented grin plastered all over your face.

Fantasy relationships can also put a bit of a hold on *real* relationships. Those that exist outside your head, that is. I seem to have developed a habit of saying no to boys who are real, simply because I think I can have more fun with someone who doesn't exist. But the truth is that no one in the real world has measured up to Darren, or indeed *any* of my make-believe men – so far. (I continue to live in hope.)

The only thing that bothers me slightly – and only very slightly – is the contented complacency I seem to have settled into. I mean, a few years ago I was a normal, angst-ridden teenager who would happily cry myself to sleep, my heart in agony over the knowledge that the chosen love of my life would never really be mine. Now, I don't seem to give a damn. This leads me to believe that, if I ever do achieve my little-house-by-the-sea, I could quite happily live there for ever on my own. At least that's what it would look like to visitors.

In reality, or at least in *my* reality, the place would be bustling. And Darren would have his own private training pitch.

Elly Baker

Contributors' Notes

Julia Austin was born in Java, Indonesia, and now lives with her family in London. She is thirteen and she plays the Gamelan, the piano and classical and electric guitar. Pearl Jam and Mudhoney are her favourite two groups at the moment.

Elly Baker is eighteen and just about to stop living with her younger brother Andrew, and her mum and step-dad. She is going to Sheffield to study History at the university there. She enjoys music, particularly Robyn Hitchcock, and she is a great fan of Ipswich Town Football Club.

Rubiya Begum was born and lived in Bangladesh until she was eight. Then she came to live in London with her parents, brothers and sisters. She is eighteen now and studying Maths, English Literature and Politics at A level. She is keen to do a Business degree and then go abroad to work. She loves watching sport on television, especially American football and ice hockey, and she also enjoys reading and drawing.

Katherine Bethell is fifteen and presently studying for her GCSEs at Islington Green Secondary School. She lives with her mum and dad and two younger brothers, who all drive her mad when they interrupt her phone calls. She plays the saxophone and enjoys art and reading and being with her friends. She particularly loves writing.

Rosie Davies lives with her mum and dad and younger sister, Molly. She sings in two choirs and is learning contemporary and Jazz dancing. She's a fan of 'Friends' and 'Eastenders' and her favourite band is Blur.

Jolene Farmer is fifteen. She was born in Scotland and moved to London when she was six. Eventually, she wants to go to art college. At the moment she is studying for her GCSEs. The main thing she enjoys is socialising with her friends. She is into music and particularly likes Blur, Supergrass, Pulp and seventies funk music.

Stacey Faulkner was born in Chatham in Kent and moved to London when she was two. She is now seventeen and studying for her A levels. She enjoys going out to the cinema with her friends and loves watching The 'X' Files on television.

Tracey Grant is eighteen and comes from Edmonton in North London. She has two older brothers and loves being an aunt to their children. She likes Swing Beat and Jungle music and going out clubbing. She is interested in black history and is just about to start at Cambridge University to study Social and Political Sciences at Kings College.

Joanna Hale is an only child and lives with her mum and dad. She is seventeen and working for her A levels. She plays the flute and the piano. She loves all types of music and particularly likes going out to see films with her friends.

Kate Highton is fifteen and lives in Hackney with her parents and her younger brother and sister. She is studying for her GCSEs and wants to carry on to do A levels. She enjoys meeting up with friends and going to clubs. She plays the violin and is a great fan of Brookside.

Kelly Indaco is seventeen. She is studying for her A levels and she eventually wants to go to university to do an English degree. She likes reading and drawing, and she is an active campaigner for animal rights.

A. J. is twenty and has one younger brother. She lives away from her family now and has been working at an English school for foreign students. She is just about to start a degree course at Leeds University studying Law and French. She hopes to be either a QC or a teacher. She enjoys athletics and reading in her spare time.

Sara Khan is a seventeen-year-old student studying for her 'A' levels. She likes cooking, and designing and making her own clothes. She listens to Indian and English music. Her favourite solo singer is Mariah Carey, and her favourite band is Eternal.

Melanie Lorene is studying A level Media, English Literature and Sociology at Hackney Sixth Form Centre. She is not sure what she wants to do after that. She likes writing poetry and listening to swing music, dance music, garage music, reggae and jazz.

Nina Miah was born in Bangladesh and brought up in Hackney. She is eighteen and about to start a law degree in Westminster University which she is excited and nervous about at the same time. She is currently trying for the gold Duke of Edinburgh Award.

Shaheena Begum Mosabbir is eighteen and has just finished her A levels at the Hackney Sixth Form Centre. She is going to study Law at The Guild Hall in London. She likes reading very much and recently she has got into ten-pin bowling. The main thing she enjoys is being around people.

Charlene Okwei-Nortey lives with her older brother Francis, her older sister Nina and her younger brother Sam. She is thirteen and goes to St Edwards School in Romford. As well as reading and writing, she enjoys swimming, riding, and all other outdoor pursuits.

Liz Pike was born in 1976 and is now nineteen. She grew up in Southend and moved to London in 1988. She has three brothers and three sisters. Her hobbies are swimming, writing poetry and listening to music. She likes Cranberries, Paul Simon, Billy Joel and Kate

Bush. She has two A levels in Media and Fine Art and after university she wants to make films.

Jessica Shaw is nineteen and lives in London. When she was three she went to live in Brazil for a year which she still remembers very clearly. She is going to Norwich soon to study Drama at the University of East Anglia. She loves music and drama, and in the future she hopes to travel as much as possible.

Laura Wasley is nineteen and studying for a degree in fashion at Bristol University. In her spare time she likes to go out clubbing, to art galleries and the cinema, and her dream is to be a fashion buyer for Harvey Nichols.